THE JOURNAL

OF

PETER RUBIN

Don't Let History Repeat Itself

By Vincent Bivona

Illustrations by Melissa Maiello

Legwork Team Publishing
New York

Legwork Team Publishing
80 Davids Drive, Suite 1
Happauge, NY 11788
www.legworkteam.com
Phone: 631-944-6511

First published by Legwork Team 9/18/2008

ISBN: 978-1-6048-1297-8 (sc)

Illustrations by Melissa Maiello

Printed in the United States of America
Bloomington, Indiana

This book is printed on acid-free paper.

Legwork Team
Publishing

This novel is

dedicated

to the ones who

cannot

seem to find an out.

Hang in there . . .

Acknowledgments

I wish to thank my mom and dad for their unyielding support, John Saviano for computer game insight, Melissa Maiello for providing illustrations, and, *most importantly,* a group of people who will remain nameless—**except to those who have inflicted their injuries first hand**—for opening wounds of the past and recounting their horrible tales of abuse.

My memories haunt me in my sleep,
They haunt me when I am awake.
Some say be thankful for what is left,
But my memories are something
I can no longer take.

I look to the sky for solace,
And I see the faces of my loved ones gone;
I try to find the jubilance I once felt,
And once again those emotions abscond.

—Diane Daniels

INTRODUCTION

Before reading any further, I would like to make it clear that everything you see before you (the derogatory statement scrawled over the words of the first entry, and the half pages which are to be interpreted as ripped pages) has been done intentionally and will be explained in time.

I also would like to make it clear that, although this is a work of fiction, it should be viewed as an actual journal, one that belongs to a boy named Peter Rubin. Keeping this in mind, I invite you to invade the sanctity of his thoughts so that you may gain a better understanding of his life.

June 21, 20--
Wednesday

It happened again.

I guess they decided they'd give me one last going away present. And although I like presents, I could have easily done without this one—my arm is still raw from the administered Indian rope burn. At least today is the last day of school, and I won't have to endure this type of treatment for the duration of the summer. Thank God. Another year of turmoil now comes to an end.

Wait. Hold on, I'm getting too far ahead. Since this is my first entry, let me start by telling you a little bit about myself. My name is Peter Rubin. I'm fourteen years old. I'm Roman Catholic. And I go to Farmsville High School. Most people I go to school with would probably describe me as "that kid," the one who has been teased and picked on as far back as anyone can remember. This isn't entirely true. There used to be a time when I had a lot of friends. There used to be a time when I had a lot of self-esteem, too. This was back in elementary school, when I hadn't a care in the world. Then something happened . . . middle school came. It all fell apart from there.

Now I'm in high school, going into tenth grade next year, and nothing has changed. I thought that when I changed schools, my reputation would change as well. But it didn't. Instead, it followed me, along with those same incessant pricks from middle school. I'll get into that later.

Since this is a journal, let me explain what I look like. I'm overweight, short for my age, and have a pasty complexion. There, I said it. There's no point masking the truth any longer. This is why I get beat up, and partially why I'm starting this journal. The only good thing I have going for me is that I don't wear glasses—at least they can't get me on that. My mom mentioned once that it was a good idea to write down your thoughts and feelings. She did it herself when she and Dad were going through a tough time, and it seemed to help her get her feelings out into the open. Since I'm not really that vocal, nor do I wish to share my thoughts with anyone other than myself, I've decided to give it a whirl. Who knows, maybe I can look back on this years from now and laugh.

A little bit more about me: I live at home with both my parents. I would like to say that they're happily married, but that would be a lie. Like I said earlier, Mom's been having some issues with Dad and has been trying to work them out. I think by Mom writing in her journal, she's actually stifling her aversion of Dad's habits. But, if it works, use it, right?

I guess I would have to describe my mom as the type of person who sort of understands me. She means well—she really does—but the generation gap inhibits conversation and understanding. I mean, hey, she *did* give me the idea for writing this journal (even if I just copied her actions), and it actually does feel better to get everything out in the open.

Anyway, my mom works for a company called Andre Fathoms Associates. It deals with investment banking. She leaves for work at five in the morning and comes home around eight at night. That's basically her life: travel to and from work, come home, eat, say hello to me and my dad, and then go to bed.

On to my dad. He's a computer stock analyst for C.V.C. Innovations. He rides the train with my mom and has a similar work schedule. He's a pretty tall guy and overweight. Sadly, I don't take after him in the vertical height, just horizontal. I take after my mom when it comes to height—the five-foot wonder. I myself am 5'4" with probably only another inch or two to go, according to the doctor. Oh, I'm Irish and Norwegian, by the way, so I guess both of my parents contributed to my pasty complexion. I didn't mention it earlier, but Rubin was actually shortened from Rubinson by my great-grandpa who came over from Norway. Search me why he changed it. That's not important. Back to my parents.

As far as my compatibility goes with them, there really is none. My dad's the older type, aged to the ripe number of fifty-six, and I have absolutely nothing in common with him. The only thing he likes to do is fish. Despite the fact that I loathe fishing, I do it every chance I get. It sucks. I'd do anything just to spend more time with him, but he never seems to have any.

The only time I really get to see him and my mom is at dinner—a punctual hour between eight and nine. They usually ask how school is, and I usually feed them the right answers, the ones they're looking for. The ones that make them happy. Just thinking about it makes my bruises ache. I wish my family was different; I'd trade their money for more time with them any day. Sometimes, I think they spend more time thinking about money than they do about me. Honestly, whose parents work on Saturday as well?

That brings me to my next topic. Since they're not home at all during the day, we have a maid. Her name is Corolla. She's a Hispanic lady, about forty-five, with long black hair and glasses. Corolla has been with us since I was nine. I had my first crush on her and went to her for advice the first time I liked a girl at school. It completely backfired, though, and I was humiliated. Stupid me. Since then, I've decided never to ask her advice again. I should have realized it wasn't worth talking to a girl in the first place. Now I just keep a friendly smile on whenever we talk. She's nice enough, cutting the ends off the peanut butter and jelly sandwiches she makes, so I don't entirely hate her, but talking to her about my problems is out of the question. Grown-ups just don't understand me.

Okay, it's getting late, and I'm pretty tired. I put this off until just before bedtime and perhaps that wasn't entirely a great idea since I'm barely staying awake. I'll write more tomorrow. I promise.

~Peter

June 22, 20--
Thursday

It's earlier now—ten p.m. on Thursday night. I feel I can stay up for a good amount of time, so I'll get more in-depth with this entry. Most kids my age would undoubtedly be going out with their friends or crashing end of school parties, like Sally Rutchfield's.

Not me.

Like I said, I'm a little different than most kids. I don't have a *bunch* of friends; I only have two: John Lombardi and Tommy "Boots" Moretti. ~~Me and John~~ John and I call him Tommy Boots because he only wears boots—a simple enough reason. Both of them are a little more outgoing than me and were invited as space-fillers. I can see through Sally Rutchfield's ruse, though. Whatever. They should have just stayed home or come over to my house. We could have played WOW (World of Warcraft). Don't get me wrong, I was invited, too, and I guess I should feel blessed for that, but nevertheless I opted not to go due to Steve Jones being there. I hope he doesn't hurt them.

Where did I leave off yesterday? Oh yeah, I was just starting out with my life. I'll talk a little bit about middle school, where I think everything went downhill. My middle school consisted of grades sixth through eighth and was conjoined with the elementary school that I had gone to as well. There's a playground in the back that I loved to swing on, but it was reserved solely for the elementary school students. Wow, thinking about all this is really a trip down memory lane. *I hate it!* But I'll go on to fill you in just the same.

Back then, I was an average size child up until the summer of sixth grade. It was then that either my metabolism changed, or I had a thyroid malfunction (and since the doctors ruled the latter out, it's probably my metabolism taking after my dad). I gained roughly thirty pounds and was the fattest seventh grader when the school year started. Corolla really should have opened her eyes. Maybe it's her fault with all those peanut butter and jelly sandwiches. It definitely didn't help my persona (the quiet child who began keeping to himself), nor did it help my self-esteem. I was teased constantly, being called "Roly-poly," "Triple Chins," "Jelly Rolls," and a bunch of other names I really don't wish to write down. One time, I even got held down while a group of kids, who I now call "The Clan," lifted up my shirt and slapped my stomach. "Jelly Rolls, Jelly Rolls," they shouted while they drummed their percussions on my stomach. Uggghh.

In response to the name-calling, my mom once told me that sticks and stones could break my bones, but words would never hurt me. I guess she never had a vocalized spear stabbed into her heart because it really does hurt. Much more than a scraped knee.

I remember hiding under the jungle gym during recess and crying. It served two purposes: it got me out of sight so those ungracious pricks couldn't further tease me, and I could also cry in peace. This was my routine until graduation, the friendless routine of having nothing to look forward to but another day of teasing and torment. I remember the playground all too well . . . it was filled with rocks. If you asked anyone who went to that school they wouldn't remember, but I would, and still do. I vividly remember the bullies throwing those rocks at me. Bullies like Steve Jones, Jordan Saunders, Casey Vector, Gary Reith, and Larry Bennerds (who thankfully didn't follow me to high school). This is The Clan I spoke of.

I used to come home with welts the size of golf balls on my head when they wailed me with a particularly large one. Once they caught up to me as I was running away and pulled me under the slide (ironically it had served as my sanctuary and at that same moment my dystopia) and threatened that if I ever told on them to Mrs. Montgomery, our principal back then, they would jump me when I got off my bus. I believed them and never said a word, just took what they dished out and lied whenever my parents caught a glimpse of a welt (if they even noticed in that one hour time slot we call dinner). I covered most of them pretty good with hats and long-sleeved shirts anyway. But when my parents did spy one and questioned me about it, I just said I fell while playing with some of my school friends.

God, I wish I had had friends back then. I didn't meet Tommy Boots and John until the end of eighth grade and I really could have used them.

That's basically how I spent middle school: hiding from the kids who beat up Peter Pumpkin Eater. Yeah, that's what Steve Jones had named me. I guess you could call him the ringleader of the group. And go figure, now John and Tommy Boots are at a party with that same person.

Whatever, I don't feel like writing anymore. I'm going to sleep.

~Peter

June 24, 20--
Saturday

Sorry I didn't write yesterday. I didn't have any time. Tommy Boots, John, and I rode our bikes down to Revina's Clutch. John said it'd be good exercise for me if I came along. It was. I nearly passed out. But it was fun, too. Maybe I'll start riding my bike a lot this summer and when tenth grade begins I'll be as fit as a fiddle. Ha ha, yeah right. But hey, I can probably lose a few pounds and not be called Roly-poly anymore. I can at least take that one thing away from them.

Let me tell you about Revina's Clutch. It's this big sand hill deposited by glaciers long ago. It's about a mile from my house and people usually use it to dump their junk in—busted red wagons, truck tires, old shelves and cabinets, etc. Aside from its unintended purpose as a dump, the kids who know about it use it as a place to ride their bikes because there's a track set up with a bunch of dirt jumps at the bottom.

When the three of us arrived, there was already a group of kids from our school there—The Clan: Jordan Saunders, Casey Vector, Gary Reith, and yup, you guessed it: Steve Jones. Just my luck. We opted to stay out of sight until they left. Even though Tommy Boots and John had seen Steve at Sally's end-of-the-year party and hadn't gotten beaten up, they're still a target for his abuse. Had it only been just the two of them that night, they would have come home with welts and wedgies—W&Ws as we got used to calling them.

After The Clan grew tired of the Clutch and left, I tried one of the jumps and nearly killed myself. I guess fat people weren't meant to fly.

When it got dark, we went for pizza and Carvel ice cream. Every time we go there, Tommy Boots mentions how cool it would be to work at an ice cream shop. All I know is that if I worked there, I would become even fatter than I already am. I'll just thank the fact that I'm still only fourteen and can't get my working papers. That reminds me, I forgot to mention that Tommy Boots is a year older than John and me, but he's still in our grade. His parents decided to hold him back in kindergarten or something.

After Carvel, we returned to Tommy Boots's house to watch *Witch Hunter*. He has the whole series on DVD. I called my mom, and she agreed to let me stay over since school was out. We watched every disk as the night progressed. When the sun breached the horizon, I settled into my sleeping bag and called it a night. What a fun day! Best thing of all: I didn't get picked on!

I remember waking up this morning to Tommy's dog licking my face. He has a cocker spaniel that he named Talitha after the main character in *Witch Hunter*. Tommy Boots's parents had gone to visit his aunt so we pigged out and tried to make breakfast ourselves. If this were a diary then the entry would surely look like this:

Dear Diary,

Today, I tried to make pancakes. Well, I did *try to make pancakes, and it* did *work! First time, too. Maybe I'll become a famous chef one day! Tommy Boots and John had theirs plain, but I loaded mine up with maple syrup. Their faces twisted in disgust when they saw how much I put on, but seriously, you can't have pancakes without maple syrup. It's an unspoken rule!*

Ha ha. After breakfast, we played WOW, which I mentioned earlier but didn't go into detail about. If you haven't played it, then I highly recommend it. The installment that we play is called "Burning Crusades" and despite the fact that neither of us played as our own Toons, John and I still had a good time trying to level Tommy Boots's. I'm probably not making any sense if you haven't played. Let me explain:

There are two main types of character choices—what we call Toons—which are the Alliance and the Horde (good guys and bad guys). My Toon is on the Horde side and is an Undead Warlock. They're so OP and everyone always QQs about it. Getting ahead of myself, aren't I? Okay, on the Alliance side there are Humans, Dwarfs, Night Elves, Gnomes—I'll stop here so I won't bore you. Each of these Toons has subcategories that you can choose from. The same goes for the Horde side with the Orcs, Undead, Taurens, Trolls, and Blood Elves. What Tommy Boots was doing was trying to make his Toon more powerful, which is done by leveling. Needless to say we succeeded, and Tommy Boots's Toon dinged sixty. I'm happy to say that my Undead Warlock is leveled out at seventy.

I could honestly fill an entire journal just about the inner workings of WOW, but I'll stop here. All I'll say is that if life was like WOW, and I had my Toons's powers, then watch out tenth grade! Peter Rubin is on the way!

One more quick fact: Ventrillo (Vent). It's this communication device that Tommy Boots, John, and I use to talk to one another while we're playing WOW. After John's parents yelled at him for taking up the phone line for hours on end, they made him get it. Now, all three of us have it.

That's pretty much it for today. Afterwards, I came home, ate dinner with my parents, and hung out with them until they went to bed. My dad asked me how my day went, and I told him it was excellent. For the first time in a long while, I *didn't* lie. Maybe I could persuade him to take a day off work to go fishing during the week, instead of only on Sundays (tomorrow we're going to try our hands at some Fluke).

I hope tomorrow brings as much fun as the past two days have.

~Peter

July 2, 20--
Sunday

Hi again. I know I haven't been writing, but the summer has been taking its toll on me. Tommy Boots, John, and I did a lot the past couple of days. We went to the mall, the ice rink, the bookstore, McCircuits (the computer store), and some festival that John's mother took us to. And today my dad and I went fishing again after church, and I caught three huge Fluke!

I'll tell you about the mall first. We like to go to the one in Bayview. (Yes, I know Sun Valley is a lot closer.) Despite the fact that the mall is almost an hour away, it's the only one I will go to for specific reasons. At least in a town an hour away, nobody knows your name, and you're free to express your life the way God intended. Nobody is marked like Cain, and nobody forks the sign of the devil or throws rocks as you go by.

John's mom usually drops us off when we go the mall. She has an aunt that lives out there, so it's really convenient for us.

I guess I could say that I love walking in the mall because it's good for you; it's a good opportunity to lose some unwanted calories. But the real reason I like the mall is the feeling it gives me, deep down inside. At the mall, unlike school, you are surrounded by people who view you as their equal, rather than a secondary piece of dog turd.

All we did at the mall was walk around, get some pizza, and look at some magazines at Waldenbooks—nothing too special, except spending a day with your friends. Something that, although it might not be that special to some, is *very* special to me.

The next day, as I said, we went to McCircuits over on Treehallow Road. It's our favorite computer store. Tommy Boots is in the process of building a supercomputer. Now don't get me wrong, he's not smart enough to hack the Pentagon, but he's a pretty good hacker (as I myself claim to be). I guess that's one plus to spending half your life at the keyboard—you learn how to do certain things.

Being a computer geek doesn't only increase your ability in hacking, it also expands your knowledge and opens you to the vast horizon of computer games.

Tommy Boots's computer has a 32" LCD television hooked up as its main monitor with two 20" Mitsubishi LCDs flanking it from both the right and left sides. His setup is really sweet and is a must-see to be truly appreciated. This is the reason we went to the store: Tommy Boots said that the video card powering his left LCD was of a poorer quality than those of his center and right and was in search of a new one.

He found it.

What's next? Oh yeah . . . the festival! Let me tell you about that! It was this big Italian fair up over on Tavern Road Park. They closed off the adjacent street and set up food venders on it. There were zepolies, calzones, heros, pizza, spaghetti . . . God, I could go on forever. I'm hungry just writing about it. Whatever pounds I lost so far, I sadly gained back.

Food—the weakness to my heart.

Inside, on the grass field, were the rides. They had the mini-roller coaster, the Zipper, crappy bumper cars, the funhouse, a bunch of others that I can't remember the names of, and the Gravitron—my favorite. The three of us rode it five times each until John emptied his stomach of any Italian pastries that had been digesting inside. That was a pretty nasty sight, but at least he held it in until he was off the ride. I don't think the grass cares about being showered in puke and ~~previously~~ pastries.

Let me tell you a little bit about the Gravitron. It's this big compartment that looks like a top. A door opens like that of a spaceship and you go inside. Inside, there are a bunch of . . . I'll call them beds. There are a bunch of these next to each other and they tilt at an angle of about eighty degrees from the floor—almost upright. Now, here's the fun part . . . they're on casters. When the ride starts the top twirls, allowing centripetal force to raise the beds. As this is happening any body or object that is in the cabin becomes plastered against them, rising as well. It's a pretty cool feeling when you're experiencing it. What's more is that there's so much force that you can even turn yourself upside down, or, if you know the balance point, stand almost parallel to the floor.

Like I said, we rode this five times until the force became too much for John and he had to get off and literally spill his guts. It was really fun.

I almost forgot to mention my fishing trip. My dad has a sixty-eight-foot Buddy Davis Sport Fisherman—it's a really nice boat. Actually, nice is not the right word to describe it and neither is boat; technically it's a yacht, and it's beautiful. It's like a house on water; it has a refrigerator, a concealed sink, a microwave, a built-in coffee maker, a bar, and a bedroom. My dad asked me if I wanted to invite Tommy Boots and John today, but I lied and told him that they were busy installing computer software. I hate to lie but is it too much to want to spend the only free time my dad has with him alone? I didn't think so, and that's what happened—it was a father and son fishing day!

That's pretty much that. I really don't want to bore you with more facts of the past week—fishing, the computer store, and the festival are more than enough—so I'll close by saying *Viva la summer!*

~Ciao, Peter

July 5, 20--
Wednesday

Yesterday was the Fourth of July and what a great day it was! Let me start by saying that both my mom and dad had off from work. *Hallelujah!* We spent the day together—the morning shooting off the fireworks my dad brought home and, after storing what we didn't blow up in the shed, the afternoon at the park.

It's always funny how you can learn something new despite your age. I'm not saying that I'm over-the-hill just yet, but being fourteen isn't the start of life either. Yesterday, I learned that Dad had asked my mom out on a date to attend a Fourth of July party about a million years ago. It was then that they shared their first kiss. They told me the story as the night sky lit up with fireworks, and it seemed to revive some dying or trapped part of their emotions for one another. It was really great to see them happy again.

The story goes as follows:

Back in college (I think my dad said it was either Berkeley or Briar Cliff), my dad had put in for a tutor. It was his second year, and as a college requirement each student had to take a language, despite their major. My dad's major was accounting. Later, he would change it to computer science when he saw that this was the way the world was moving, but back then it was accounting. That's how he got my mom as his tutor. She was an accounting major, too, except she stuck with it until the day she received her bachelor's degree.

She said that the way she was able to put extra snacks in her dorm room's refrigerator and pay for movies was by working as a language tutor—French to be specific. She had taken it in high school and passed with flying colors. Back then, her mother had told her that she had some French in their family, but she later found out that had just been a ploy to engage her in the language program. She wasn't horribly angry when she learned this little fact. In fact, she was grateful, for if it weren't for that push, she would have taken music instead, and would have never met my dad.

Well, fate played out, and my dad received her as his tutor. He said that she tutored him up until his final and he passed only because of her help. It was then that my dad fell instantly in love with her, and as he would later find out, she with him as well.

The sad thing about college is, like any other school year, it ends and the students go back home for the summer. Knowing this, my dad and my mom exchanged numbers and addresses and promised to write one another, hoping to keep up their friendship. One week before the Fourth of July, my dad wrote my mom and asked her to come and celebrate the holiday with him and his family—my dad said that back then the Fourth of July was always a family-driven holiday, one with an endless amount of food (I would have fit right in)—and she replied that she would. Their towns weren't terribly far away, so it must have been fate. She visited. He introduced her to everyone. And at the end of the night, they shared their first kiss under the fireworks.

A true romance story. I hope I have the same college experience and find the love of my life as well. It's just sad the way they fight sometimes now. It seems that they forgot just how heart-strung they were for one another back then. Even so, the telling of that story seemed to rekindle some long-lost flame. Maybe the future will hold the rest of the antidote to whatever illness wriggled its way into their hearts.

I don't mean it to sound like they have a hatred for one another. I just hope that the rekindled flame doesn't go out. I hope it acts like those trick candles that sit atop a birthday cake. Speaking of which, mine's next month: August tenth.

The big one-five.

~Peter

July

Hey, its me again.

Just thought I'd write has been happening since the doing such things like this. It and has been through it all with the single

It was a really hot day the tree at the end of the path pickings. I had three myself not even sour! That reminds to; they had jelly apples that least I brush my teeth every think I might have to go to the

Another thing that we did by the cliff and threw rocks skipped at least five times by making it seem like it sh bounced. Mine sank as I tho Boots's didn't. His went all end. I couldn't believe it! I would.

That's when I took the hand and went over

go to the park and art—and wooden bat a fake one that we go pied by the real players. my dad had put me on a to stand out in the outfield the white particles drifting ferent; I don't mind that nted pounds, especially if went out and had a good John had to go home. nd I'll be writing more that this summer lasts.

July 15, 20--
Saturday

Hey! Summer is going great! Tommy Boots, John, and I went to the beach today after church, and the water was fantastic. You would probably have to have a recapitulation of the weather to truly appreciate the cool water. For the past week the temperature has been in the nineties, and rain has seemed to boil out of existence. Now, knowing this, the water felt great!

You're probably wondering about my appearance at the beach. And by me writing that I had such a great time there you would most likely think that I'm over my self-consciousness. Sadly, this is not the case and probably never will be. Since middle school I've been wearing a large T-shirt to the beach and whenever I go in pools. It hides a lot, and since it's baggy it doesn't really stick to my skin when it's wet—only when I come out of the water, and if I pull on it or ring it out, it does its job of concealment. The wearing of the shirt also provides another use—I don't have to put on sunblock. I hate the sticky feeling anyway, and with my pale complexion, if I didn't wear any I'd probably roast.

I've shared my reasoning why I wear what I wear to the beach, and neither Tommy Boots nor John say anything about it. They realize what I go through. They even go through it themselves, but not as much and never due to them being fat (they're both ectomorphic in appearance).

Tommy Boots and I buried John. This is one of the many things we always do at the beach. Consider it a tradition. It always starts out by one of us digging a hole, then winds up escalating to one of us jumping inside and having the others fill it in. Today, it was John who jumped in. I would have—I haven't gotten buried in over two summers—if I could have fit in the hole, but due to my overly large mid-section, I couldn't. It's sad, but you have to look at the positives: if I can't be the one buried, than being the burier is best to none.

We almost had a fright as well. When we buried John, we buried him up to his neck—the hole being at least four feet deep, and with him scrunching his legs, he managed to get down that far. Then, the water started to come in. John's mom had dropped us off and said she'd pick us up in five hours, making the pickup at about four p.m. The tide came in at three.

The beach we go to doesn't have lifeguards. It sounds bad, but it's not one of those huge public beaches, it's more or less a shoreline where people gather to sunbathe, jog, or cast out their fishing lines. (What? You actually thought I'd go to a public beach?) There's about twenty feet of uncovered sand to lie on when it's low tide. When it's high, there is only about twelve, the ocean swallowing eight feet—roughly forty percent. It just so happened to be that it was within these eight feet that John was buried.

We always leave the buried person in the hole for at least an hour; it's a game we play. If the buried person can't bear it then we dig them out, and they have to buy the ice cream. If they win, then they are the one to be treated, not once, but twice that upcoming week.

Seeing the tide come in, Tommy Boots and I had to call off all bets. John had been facing us—toward the land—and lucky for him, too, because if he hadn't, then I think the inside of that hole would have been brown by the time we dug him out—the tide nearly reached the back of his head before we noticed it was coming in.

Nevertheless, we got him out, and just in time. The water crashed at the back of his head two or three times, and, on the return, slapped him against the front of his face like a fist. I don't think I will ever forget his face the first time the water went rushing past him: it was complete terror. How I wish it could have been Steve Jones in his place. I think I might have actually watched him drown.

All and all, it was another great day! I didn't get picked on, and hey, maybe, just maybe, I'll get some kind of a farmer's tan and not burn like usual. As the motto of the New York Lottery states: *Hey, you never know!*

Birthday count down: Twenty-six days!!!

~Peter

July 24, 20--
Monday

Wow, time's flying. Sorry that I'm not writing that much, but I'm really tired when I get home. Sometimes I stay over Tommy Boots's or John's house, and I don't bring you with me. I think I'd die of embarrassment if they read my thoughts. I mean, yeah, we share our feelings with one another on a few things, but most of what I have written in here is personal—personal things that will be taken to the grave.

Since my last entry, I've gone to the beach again, went to the mall about three more times, and started reading a short story called *I Am Legend.* I haven't finished it yet, but it seems really interesting so far; almost seems to me like it's portraying a twisted reality of my life. The main character, a man by the name of Robert Neville, is seemingly the last person on the earth. Well, the last *human* person on the earth, but that's not where the relevance lies—it lies in the fact that he's forced to be a loner. When a swarm of vampires inhabit the earth that would be my guess on what would happen. Nevertheless, the vampires resemble The Clan, and I resemble Robert Neville. They are the evil, and I am the last man alive who must avoid falling prey to their wrath. I'm sure more similarities will present themselves as I finish the story.

Despite the amount of time I spend in my house during

the school year, I never really took up reading that much. I mostly found myself tinkering away on the computer, studying, or browsing some science fiction comics—they're all my escape into another world. Now things might be different. I think I might actually get a library card and check out a few new books after I finish this anthology.

It's actually kind of odd how I came to read the book in the first place. Since my parents are out from four-thirty a.m. to eight p.m. during the week, and Corolla's shift is usually from noon to six, there's that two-hour period where the house is empty. It was within these two hours that I found myself, armed with a Nerf gun, pretending I was Agent 007. John was Alec Trevelyan (Agent 006), and Tommy Boots was Dr. No. For some reason, John likes the old Bond movies and always pretends he is 006. He also makes us watch them whenever we sleep over at his house.

That's how the setup went, and since I was Bond, they were both after me. We usually switch it up every now and then, but since I'm the best with a Nerf gun (maybe I'll become a cop one day due to my shooting skills), we usually play two versus one. More specifically, them versus me.

Where was I? Oh, yeah . . . I was hiding from 006 and Dr. No. They were hot on my pursuit and followed my trail into the complex (my kitchen). Knowing that they would do this, I ducked behind a steel drum (the den couch) for safety. When I spied that double-crossing agent, 006, maneuvering and over-exaggerating his way into the weapons room, I popped up from behind my barricade and began ripping loose a barrage of Nerf darts.

006 tucked and rolled behind a bulletproof safe (the recliner) while, behind him, Dr. No. let loose two darts before taking cover behind the wall. I dodged every one of those speeding bullets but was struck in the head by something as one of them ricocheted off the wall. In reality, it was actually one of my dad's books that was wounded instead of the wall, and that's what staggered off the shelf and clobbered me. The book, of course, being the anthology by Richard Matheson. I ignored the book, pushing it under the couch, and finished the game by flanking 006 and bunkering Dr. No. As I said earlier: superior shooting skills. I got my congratulations, retrieved my dad's book, and we all took five for food.

Birthday countdown: Seventeen days!!!

~Peter

August 2, 20--
Wednesday

I can't believe it's August already. It's both a good and bad thing. Good because my birthday is coming up, and bad because that means school is right around the corner and I have to see *them* again. Maybe things will be different this year.

Over dinner tonight, both my mom and dad asked me what I wanted for my birthday, and I replied that I wanted nothing in particular, just to spend time with them. Since my birthday is going to fall on a Thursday this year, my wish would be impossible. It's not a total loss—they did say they would do something with me on the thirteenth, instead, since it will be a Sunday. I know it's a little disheartening, but at least we can spend the whole day together—just me and them.

That's another thing about my parents: even though they have Sunday off, they seldom spend it with me. I have written that Sunday is the one day my dad usually tries to go fishing—and I join him every time I can—but he doesn't do it as often as he wishes. He's usually tired, and both my mom and him say it's their only day to sleep in and to catch up on their sanity. Sometimes, more often than not, my dad even has work to do on his laptop. He says that those numbers aren't going to crunch themselves.

When I grow older, and someday have a family of my own, I'm not going to be like my parents and be obsessed with my work. Money isn't everything, and I'll gladly trade wealth for family bonding anytime.

Back to my birthday:

I think I might ask them to take me out to dinner. I have some time to decide where, but I'm leaning toward Kotakamo. It's this sushi place down on Main Street where Tommy Boots and I went for John's birthday. If you don't know what sushi is, then I'll let you in on a little secret. It's raw fish!

I know, I know, sounds nasty right? Nope! Completely the opposite. I was leaning toward the former thought myself, thinking that I'd never eat something uncooked (the rarest I take my steak is well-done), but John kept nagging me to try a spicy-tuna roll, and I did just to shut him up. I can say from that moment on, I became a raw fish fanatic. I remember how I ordered two rolls and three pieces of sashimi—which is just another name for the slices of raw fish—after savoring the taste of that one spicy-tuna roll.

Since then, I've been dreaming about going back. My mom hates raw fish, but my dad loves it. That's one thing I found out during our hour-long dinner conversation. I guess I take after him on that.

~~And I'm glad that him and I can~~

It's good to know we have *something* in common.

In any case, that's where I want them to take me. Also, I

think Tommy Boots and John are going to do something on my actual birthday. They haven't said what yet, but I have a feeling it's going to involve an archaic VHS of 007.

Birthday countdown: Eight days!!!

~Peter

August 10, 20--
Thursday

I'm fifteen now! I've survived yet another year of ducking under the bar!

The day began with me waking up to Corolla's peanut butter and jelly sandwiches (the crust cut off of course) for breakfast. It had been intended to be a lunch for me, but since I stayed up late at John's house last night, it ended up being my breakfast. It didn't matter anyway; I love peanut butter and jelly, and I can have it any time of the day. After breakfast, Corolla handed me a card from her, and one from my mom and dad as well.

In Corolla's was a Simon gift certificate redeemable at any Simon mall. Bless her for that ambiguous choice—God only knows what I'd do if it were only for Sun Valley. In my mom and dad's was nothing but a short squib saying how proud they were of me turning fifteen, and that it was a special age—it was one year away from sixteen. I guess that's why the girls have their sweet sixteen parties; it's *their* special age. I've heard plenty of hoopla about these from the older girls in the hall last year to know it's the one birthday they'll never forget. So important that they have a huge party where hundreds of their friends attend to share in the festivities. I didn't hold my breath hearing this nor will when school commences again—

I'll never be invited to one of them. Tenth grade will be devoid of festivities.

Corolla had said that even though my parents didn't put anything in the card it didn't mean they didn't love me and weren't planning to do something later when they got home. At the time, I thought the former, but when they came home it turned out to be the latter—they had actually gotten me something.

During the day, Tommy Boots and John came over. Each of them brought a small gift, which I immediately opened. John's was the new Air Max Nerf gun, fifteen shots of rapid-fire dart suction! Tommy Boots's was a collectable deck of the *Witch Hunter* series cards. Inside were instructions for three different types of games you could play with the deck, and if another was purchased, a fourth. We spent the remainder of the afternoon learning each of the three games and mastering them.

After watching the Thursday night episode of *Witch Hunter*, my parents came home. Dad seemed overly jubilant at the fact that his son had turned fifteen and embraced me in a warm bear-type fatherly hug. I accepted it with great gratitude, wishing it didn't have to end. A moment later, my mom duplicated his actions and gave me one as well. It sounds childish—and I don't care—but I could have stayed in their arms forever. That would have been the best gift I could have ever received.

The plan was to spend the night at John's house where the three of us would stay up all night watching another old 007 movie—this one being Goldfinger, where John would fantasize about being Auric Goldfinger. But first was my birthday cake.

I sent Tommy Boots and John ahead of me to "prepare" for the sleepover. My parents said they could have stayed, but I don't think I can be labeled selfish if I want to spend the remainder of the one hour I get with my parents alone.

To conclude, dinner was great. We had corn beef and cabbage, and afterwards my mom pulled out a Carvel ice cream cake that she must have hidden somewhere other than the freezer. I know this because I roved in there for a snack earlier and didn't find anything out of the ordinary.

The cake was delicious, and between my dad and I, we finished the whole thing. God bless vanilla ice cream. My mom also presented me with a Borders gift card for fifty dollars.

A good day indeed.

Birthday countdown: 364 days!!! (Just kidding.)

~Peter

August 13, 20--

Sunday

Today was great. The sermon at church was fun, and since it's a Sunday, my mom and dad took me out to Bellport to visit my cousins. I think they did it more for their own reasons than mine, but that doesn't bother me; I still got to see my family.

It's a rarity that I get to see Joey and Melissa and their parents—Uncle Patrick and Aunt Lisa—and whenever we do, it's always a fun gathering. This time they took us out to this restaurant called Mama Leone's. It's this Italian place, and although I'm Irish and Norwegian, I loved every bit of it. My Uncle Patrick said that they'd been going to it for years and know the owner personally, even have a special discount card since they're such frequent customers.

The owner hooked us up; he pushed two tables together in the back and let us in without having to wait. I saw Uncle Patrick shake the man's hand, and when he pulled it away, I could have sworn a folded bill appeared in it before the man heatedly stashed it into his pocket. I think that's so cool. I have to practice it some day.

I ordered the calamari (I think that's how you spell it). It was my first time tasting it, and Uncle Patrick said that I'd love it. He was right; the flavor just burst in my mouth.

Over dinner, we all pretty much caught up on family events. My dad told Aunt Lisa how his job was going, and my mom did the same with Uncle Patrick. Parent talk is so boring. Joey, Melissa, and I talked about *Witch Hunter* instead. They're both avid fans and haven't missed a single episode yet. It's really cool to have something in common with your cousins. While we were waiting for the food to be served—the worst part of going out to eat I think (I always starve while the anticipation sets in)—I cracked out the *Witch Hunter* cards Tommy Boots got me. We played a game and a half before we were served and another four when we returned to their house.

There, we watched old family videos, as tradition follows, then pretty much just sat around. From our spot on the floor in the adjacent room we could hear our parents yabbering away about things which seem so trivial to us. Stock portfolios, liquidating assets, blah!

That's pretty much it. We returned home at ten and I'm writing now at ten-thirty p.m. It's too late to go out so I think I'll see what's happening on WOW.

~Peter

August 22, 20--
Tuesday

This sucks! Only thirteen more days of summer vacation left, and then school starts again. I really thought that the summer was going to last longer but as my mom says: *Time flies when you're having fun.* Consequently, the same goes for the antithesis: school is going to crawl by at a sloth-like speed.

Just watch.

All summer long I haven't seen The Clan—save for that one day at Revina's Clutch, but they didn't see me so I guess that doesn't count—but in school what are the odds of that happening?

Slim to none. Those are the odds. They're going to find me, and they're going to pick on me. Uhh!!

I hate school.

I hate my life.

~Peter

August 25, 20--
Friday

Reading what I wrote the other day, it seems that I was a little upset. And who could blame me? Summer has been going great and now it all winds down to expecting nothing but the worst at school.

Sure, I might have jumped the gun when I wrote what I did. I mean it *could* be possible that Steve Jones and those disciples of his have changed for the better. Then again, it could have been possible that I lost weight over the summer and that *didn't* happen. So I guess we'll see. But for now it's best to play things by ear, hoping for the best and preparing for the worst. That's my life's motto I guess. At least in that respect, if things take a turn for the worst, I wont be totally down and out.

~Peter

August 30, 20--
Wednesday

The gap is really closing now. Only five more days left. My parents seem excited for me. I wish *I* was. They seem to think I am at least, so that's good.

They keep on saying, *"Look how our Peter Rabbit is growing up!"*

Tenth grade.

Looking on the bright side of things all I have to do is get though this year, the next, and the one after and I'm scot-free! (Steve free is more like it!)

I always hear people talking, and I've read on plenty of online forums that college is the start of a new life. You arrive with a clean slate, and nobody knows you from a hole in the wall. There was even this really old movie called *The New Guy* that portrayed the same theme, but in high school. In the movie, the kid—I forgot his name—had a similar situation as mine, but not as bad, and to make things better he had moved and started over in a new school with a new image and persona—a biker.

A rough, tough, carved from steel biker.

I doubt my parents would move, and I don't think I could pull off being a biker, but just the same, college could really be my way out. It would be the start of a new Peter Rubin.

. . . *Pete* R.

Yeah . . .

~Peter

September 3, 20--
Sunday

Oh, God, school starts tomorrow. It's really here, and this isn't a dream; it really starts tomorrow. I even said a prayer in church today, in hopes that this year will be better than the others.

The past two days, Tommy Boots, John, and I have been doing back-to-school shopping. My dad gave me a fifty-dollar bill and said that it should be ample funds to accrue what I need. *Ample, Accrue:* definitely my dad's books leaking into his vocabulary. I guess it'll soon happen to me as well, since I've been reading a lot more now. Looking back, I see that some new words have surfaced in my writings already, despite the fact that I had what I thought was a pretty good vocabulary to begin with. Maybe I'll skip out on being a cop and become a writer instead. At least in that sense I wouldn't be shot at.

The first place the three of us went was to Staples over on Grover Ave. It's a big store with a whole bunch of office supplies. They have chairs, desks, printers, and computers. You name it. Their computers really aren't that good, though. You have to go to McCircuits over on Treehallow for that. At Staples, I picked up a Five Star five-subject notebook, along with a new Trapper Keeper (I had to throw out my old one on the last day of school so my parents wouldn't see it—that dullard Steve Jones drew a big reproductive organ on it and wrote choice words under his art work).

Tommy Boots also picked up a Five Star notebook, his being blue instead of my green. We joked about how if John had gotten a red one then we could have been the three chipmunks, but that definitely would have given those jerks something to pick on us about. Instead, John had gotten a blue one as well. The two blues vs. the green!

John and Tommy Boots also had to get Trapper Keepers, but wanted to go to Circuit City because they had the *Witch Hunter* series Trappers. The ones with an image from one of the episodes on the front cover. I would have gotten that, of course, but I know it would only be destroyed. I think Tommy Boots and John understood, although I didn't really come right out and say it. I had just said that I wanted a plain black one this year.

That's basically what we got at Circuit City, and that was on the second day of our little expedition to find the school supplies. I almost forgot to mention that at Circuit City we also had to pick up a TI-83 model graphing calculator. Since the three of us will be in accelerated math this year, we have to start plotting graphs via calculators. How? I don't know, but I'm up for the challenge. I think it'll be really cool. Now, we'll have the most technological calculators in our grade!

Well, wish me luck, tomorrow is D-day for me.

Hope for the best, prepare for the worst, right?

~Peter

P.S. I almost forgot to mention that, although we've had our schedules for the past month, we haven't compared our classes. We thought it might be fun this year to let fate intervene and surprise us.

September 4, 20--
Monday

It could have gone worse. That's all I'll say. I don't mean to make it sound like anything horrible happened—it didn't. But it can only set the stage for something in the future.

I can feel it.

First off, Tommy Boots and John weren't in as many of my classes as I'd hoped. Second, The Clan made a reappearance into my life.

Let me tell you about my classes, before I explain what I'm talking about.

First period I have Math, which is likewise my homeroom. Homeroom is just a fancy name for the allotted time where the school takes the general attendance and dictates the messages that inform the student body of the events on that particular day—say an assembly or shortened periods consequential to that assembly.

Last year, I remember John telling me that the school had announced a fun day. It figures I was home sick. I remember this because Steve had been absent the next day. His followers don't pick on me too much without him to nudge them along. Just shows how much of a *cohort* (new word I learned today) they are, ones with one solitary mind—his.

I got off track, sorry. As I was saying, first period is Math, and I have that with Mr. Rugerdy. He seems like he's going to be a good teacher. He's very energetic and came right out and said that we're going to have fun in his class, so don't go falling asleep on him. I respect teachers and wouldn't even think of it. Steve isn't in that class, only Gary Reith (I honestly don't know how he managed to get into an AP class), so it won't be too bad. As I said earlier: when they're broken apart, The Clan doesn't really badger me.

Second period, I have AP Chemistry with Mrs. Pastorelli. I've had her for AP Bio. last year, so I'm sure this year's going to be a blast. I took a seat right up front so I don't miss anything. I like her because she shows lots of videos—at least in AP Bio. she did. I doubt there will be a lot of videos for Chemistry. We'll probably get to do a lot of cool experiments instead. I remember seeing a bunch of kids last year coming out of the Chem. rooms with silver pennies and silver-coated glass bottles. I think this is going to be the best period of the day because of that, and because both Tommy Boots and John are in there, too. They sit next to me. And once again, no Steve!!!

Third period I have either the lab portion of Chem. or Gym class. The way the school day works out is that it's broken up into "A" days and "B" days. On the "A" days I have the lab portion of Chemistry, where we're actually going to be doing the experiments, and on the "B" days I have Gym class, where we'll be switching off on activities throughout the year. Since today was an "A" day, we had the lab portion of the class, and we got started on the introduction of the periodic table of elements. Tomorrow we'll begin Gym class, and we'll probably be choosing the first of the activities for this quarter.

Fourth period I have Social Studies with Mr. Clemmings. He's tall, skinny, and bald. I haven't seen him around school before, but that's probably because he hangs out in the sophomore wing. I swear his head is so shiny you could see the reflection of the fluorescents overhead.

I hope *I* never lose my hair.

I sit next to John in this class, and of course with every good thing comes a bad: Steve's in this class, along with two of his drones: Jordan Saunders and Casey Vector. They sit on the opposing side of the room—I made sure of this—and they haven't done anything to me . . . yet, only called me Pony-boy.

Yea cause you're a Rolly Polly!

I don't even know what that means.

Whatever.

John will keep me company.

What am I up to now? Fifth period, that's right. Fifth period I have dum . . . dum . . . dum . . . dum . . . Lunch! My favorite class. Just joking. But you have to eat. And by fifth period today, I exhibited a voracious display of food consumption. I bet you can guess what I ate, too. Yup, peanut butter and jelly with the ends cut off.

This period has a trade-off from the one before it. Tommy Boots sits with me, while John's stuck in Math with the other math teacher, Mrs. O'hera. I'll take the trade-off; Tommy Boots is awesome, and I'm glad at least one of my best friends is with me. I just wish both of them could have had the same lunch period like last year. I guess it was a hit or miss. It could have been worse—the school splits up the tenth, eleventh, and twelfth grades into three lunch periods: fifth, sixth, and seventh, so we each could have been confined to seclusion. *"Them's the breaks,"* as my dad said over dinner tonight when he asked about my schedule. The thing about high school lunch is that there is no recess. When I first found this out last year, I was pretty upset, but when I realized that it would make it harder for The Clan to pick on me, I praised it. The lunch period isn't completely devoid of physical activity like I'm describing it to be—we're allowed to go outside the cafeteria into the courtyard and play handball, but that's about it. Be that as it may, I think I'll be staying inside and hailing sanctuary like Quasimodo.

Sixth period I have English with Jordan Saunders and Casey Vector. Tommy Boots and John are on the other side of the school in the language labs, where they both take Italian with Mr. Terzelli. The absolute worse thing about this period is that Mrs. Foxwood assigned our seats by alphabetical order, and guess who sits behind me. Yup, you guessed it; Jordan

Saunders. Arggg! I can't win. Today he only poked me in the back with his pen and told me that we were going to have a wonderful year together, and maybe, just maybe, if I wrote his essays for him, he'd leave me alone.

I think I'll become a writing machine this year.

Next comes seventh period, where I make *my* way to the Language Labs. I saw Tommy Boots and John on my way—I guess we'll be intersecting at the same point every day, which is cool—and I told them about my misfortune of sitting in front of Jordan. They both sympathized for me. Tommy Boots even called him a Sally-boy Prick. Ha ha! I love Tommy Boots!

I chose French again, like last year, to follow in my dad's footsteps. It's the second year of the four-year requirement, and it's pretty cool. Apparently none of the bullies are smart enough to engage themselves in a foreign language. Thank God! The teacher who teaches this class is Mrs. Rugerrielli. She seems nice, but is also very strict. And, oh yeah . . . I'm not quite sure how to put this, so I'll just come right out and write it: There's a beautiful girl that sits in front of me. Oh, God, I'm blushing. I thought only girls do that. When we went through attendance, I found out her name is Katie Murgelsy, and she is new to the school district, originally coming from a town called Leehaven.

Katie . . .

I know what they mean now when they say you've been

struck by Cupid's arrow. I doubt I'll ever find the courage to talk to her. Mrs. Rugerrielli said that we're going to be doing a lot of group projects in her class so maybe, just maybe, I'll get paired up with her!

After French, I have Health with Mr. Cane, and sadly, Katie isn't in that class. I got there extra early and took a seat on the left-hand side, hoping I'd get to watch her auburn hair sway in the air as she came walking through the door. But I didn't. Instead, I got to see the sour pucker of Steve Jones's face and the sarcastic sneer of Gary Reith's. After them, John thankfully strode through the door in that familiar fashion of his—maybe it's the weight of his backpack (he refuses to use his locker and totes all his books with him). At least with him in the class, I won't have to endure the wrath of half The Clan all by myself.

We're supposed to be learning a lot about the sexual reproduction system in Health. It sounds a little nasty, but I guess it's good to learn about what's going on "down there." At the mention of "sexual organs," both Steve and Gary laughed. A few of the girls around them giggled. How do girls like them? I don't understand it!

Last, but not least, is ninth period. I originally had a free, but knowing that I'd be a sitting duck if John or Tommy Boots wasn't with me, I decided to fill it with an elective. There's nothing worse than being stuck in the cafeteria alone when one of The Clan might have a free as well. By the way, a "free" is a free period of which you don't have a class. In the case of a free, you get to sit in the cafeteria and study, talk, and relax. I usually opt to do my homework.

The elective I chose to fill my free with was Home Economics, or Home Ec. for short. It's only a half-year elective, but it'll fill most the gap in my schedule. I had a choice of choosing either Home Ec. or Cinematography, and although Cinematography sounds really cool, I'd rather cook. I get hungry towards the end of the day. Oh yeah! Guess who's in my Home Ec. class? Yup! Katie Murgelsy. So it was a good choice after all! She sits on my diagonal, two rows over. Mrs. Turner, the teacher, stated that we wouldn't be static for long anyway. We just have to learn the basics of cooking and sewing, before we engage in the given lesson.

That pretty much sums up my day. Like I said earlier, I wish I had more classes with Tommy Boots and John, but I guess these will have to suffice. At least there's Katie to look forward to seeing every day. That at least should provide me with some drive to endure the thrashings of The Clan.

Speaking of which, the thing that can only set the stage for something bad in the future is the fact that I got called down into the guidance office. It wasn't the trip in itself but rather what my counselor, Mr. Gordon, told me. He said that due to Home Ec. only being a half-year course, and because of my free period and my enhanced grades, he would like to bestow upon me the privilege of being a hall monitor during the third and fourth quarters.

I know it sounds like a great honor, but ninth period is when all the older jocks try to leave early, calling from their cell phones and signing themselves out, sneaking into the parking lot and hopping the fence. And guess who has to make sure they have a pass?

Me.

I'm not the type of person to tell a teacher no, but I wish I could have been.

It's only going to set the stage for something bad. I can feel it. I'm sure there are plenty of older Steves around.

~Peter

September 5, 20--
Tuesday

Day two coming to a close.

It went okay. I can't really describe it as anything else. We started our introduction on matrices in Math, and Mr. Rugerdy assigned page ten for homework. Nothing too hard; I took care of it in lunch so I wouldn't have to lug my math book home. That reminds me of another thing: I have bad luck. Maybe horrible luck. The one free period of the day (excluding ninth period, the second half of the year), and I have to share it with Steve Jones. I thought that after yesterday without seeing him, I was Steve-free, but nope, I wasn't.

The way our cafeteria is built, it has the center corral—where you pick up and pay for your food—and two conjoining, but separate, lunchrooms. I sit with Tommy Boots in the smaller one that's been deemed the west wing cafeteria. Yesterday, Steve must have been sitting in the east wing because I saw him today while waiting in line to pay. Corolla had packed me the numero uno sandwich (peanut butter and jelly) but I had finished it, was still hungry, and decided to get a hot pretzel. There were maybe ten kids behind him in line—including myself—and thankfully he didn't see me . . . yet. I wonder how long I can keep that up for.

I almost forgot to mention that, since it was a "B" day,

we had Gym instead of the lab portion of Chem. and guess who was in my class. Go on, I'll give you three guesses. Yup. Steve Jones.

Steve didn't do anything to me, and when he saw me the next period in Social Studies, he and his buddies looked at me and laughed, but that was all; no physical abuse.

Tommy Boots really made me laugh in Chem. class, which, when I think about it, put me in a cheery mood. We were going over the periodic table of elements when he let out a huge fart! Everybody in the class burst out into laughter, and Mrs. Pastorelli—laughing as well—asked him if he could explain himself. In response he said, *"I guess I had a build up of atomic numbers one, seven, and eight on that chart there."* It was hilarious; the class erupted further into laughter, and a few kids actually fell out of their chairs! Mrs. Pastorelli surprisingly gave Tommy Boots extra credit points for his explanation, stating that it had been "very scientific."

And then, there was Katie. Katie Murgelsy.

Mrs. Rugerrielli assigned each of us to a character in the role-play from *French in Action: Continued.* I was some guy named Seaton, who, from my understandings of the story, was the brother-in-law of Adora (Katie). I wish I'd had the role of Beau, Adora's husband, instead, because Mrs. Rugerrielli was really into this particular story and made us turn our desks into a circle and act out the feelings of the characters. I got to say about a half a page to Katie in all, but in that brotherly fashion. Although I didn't get to hold those lustrous eyes in my sight as long as I had wanted to, I still got to interact with her, and was thankful. So what if I was under a façade? I still got to talk to her! I was on cloud nine until Health, which consequently was the next period, where Steve Jones started up his taunting, calling me Pony-boy again. Was he referring to *The Outsiders*? I have no idea. I can only imagine what will come this year. He couldn't say too much more to me anyway; after John stepped into the room—five seconds before the bell rang—Mr. Cane started the class, telling us about the importance of condoms and all the STDs they protect you from.

Lastly, as usual, I had Home Ec., and the fortune to see Katie again. She didn't talk to me, but I got to watch her talk to her new friend, Sarah Kimble. I wonder what would have happened if I sat next to her?

Maybe I'll find out tonight in my dreams.

~Peter

Keep dreaming Pony boy!

September 6, 20--
Wednesday

Hey, I know this is a little different with me writing upon waking, instead of before going to bed, but I couldn't sleep, and I have about an hour to kill. My parents are already out of the house, most likely on the train, so I can't spend time with them. Maybe I'll wake up an hour earlier tomorrow and we can all have breakfast together, but for now let me write.

So far, so good with school. I don't feel as depressed as I did last year, and I guess that's because Steve Jones and his friends—The Clan—haven't really started their tormenting yet. Maybe this year they've grown up and matured. I'm sure the fact that they're not all together in one class has something to do with it, and I'm downright happy for that. I just hope it lasts.

What I really want to write about, though, is Katie. I can't get her off my mind. I know I've only seen her twice, but she's not like anyone I've ever met before. Well, not met, but seen, you know what I mean. I see how she talked and joked around with Sarah, and she seems like she's got a great head on her shoulders, a persona that will enthrall anyone with a Y chromosome.

I guess what I really want to say is that I hope she doesn't fall in with the wrong crowd. I know how girls are at this age in life, and how finding a steady boyfriend is the most important thing on their minds, but when coming to a new school, you're not too familiar with all the cliques. What if she ends up with Steve or Gary, or any other members of The Clan? I guess that's what I'm really afraid of. That they'll turn her from one of those good girls into one of those Plastics (counterfeits), the ones who snarl their snide remarks at me through their gritted teeth. What did I ever do to them? Why am I thinking like this anyway? Do I really think she's going to have a crush on me? Ha! I wish . . .

I really *do* wish, though.

If I could have someone like her to share my thoughts with, maybe some things would begin to go right. Maybe people would treat me with respect, and I could actually *speak* my thoughts instead of just writing them in this journal.

And maybe pigs will fly.

I can still pray to St. Christopher and ask my guardian angel for guidance. There's always hope in this world and that's the most important thing.

I'm going to go make some breakfast now; my stomach is growling. A few bowls of Rice Krispies should change that.

Wish me luck at school today.

~Peter

September 7, 20--
Thursday

Today John almost got into a fight. It was fourth period, during Mr. Clemmings's class, when it happened. I was already sitting down waiting for John and Mr. Clemmings to come in, when Casey Vector came over and punched me in the arm. It only hurt a little, but I made it out like it hurt more so maybe he'd feel like he succeeded in something and leave me alone. It almost worked, I guess. He called me Pony-boy again and walked away. Jerk.

Here's the thing though, when Casey was hitting me and calling me names, he must have really been doing it as more of a distraction, because that's when John walked into the room and was tripped by Jordan Saunders. I don't know how I wasn't the main target today, but I wasn't. Today, it was John. I only had a split second to glace up and see him go sprawling to the floor, banging his knee, and spilling the papers out of his *Witch Hunter* Trapper Keeper before I could make sense of what had just occurred.

That's when the unthinkable happened: John stood up and pushed Jordan back. Something I would never do. A few kids sitting down turned around and shouted: *"Ohhhh."* But before Jordan could do anything, Mr. Clemmings walked into the room and asked if there was a problem. From across the room, Steve gave John the evil eye, and John said that there wasn't, that he just tripped. I was scared for him for the rest of the day, and thankfully nothing happened. I think The Clan might be planning something, though. Guys like Jordan Saunders don't let plebs like us show retaliation. It gives their rep a bad name, and the other kids already saw what John did. Something's coming; I can feel it.

After Social Studies, I kept a lookout for The Clan, making sure they didn't start anything or try to sneak up on John. In English, Jordan poked me in the back with his pencil—it was the sharpened end—and said that John was going to get it when he least expected it. I kept my mouth shut to that comment, only winced as the point of the pencil tunneled its way deeper into my left shoulder.

During lunch, Steve noticed the table we were sitting at. He must have been taking a stroll to the guidance office, and I wasn't really paying enough attention to duck when he came—I was too busy talking to Tommy Boots about the last *Witch Hunter* episode. That's when Steve came over and pushed my head into my peanut butter and jelly sandwich. Tommy Boots said something to him, but he only laughed and walked away. Jerk. Needless to say, I spent the rest of the period trying to pick peanut butter out of my nose. Now that he knows that we sit on the west side, he's apt to come back and start more trouble.

I don't want to close this entry on a bad note, so let me say something about Katie. She was wearing a halter-top today and blue-striped shorts. They weren't long and came down about halfway between her waist and knee, which allowed them to show a lot of her legs, which are smooth and tan, as if she'd spent the summer at the beach. I can't tell you how crazy that drove me.

In Home Ec., we got to move around and take inventory at our stations, which reminds me: I forgot to mention that the class was split into five groups of five kids, arranged in alphabetical order. And with that being said, I curse my last name. If only I'd been born a Martin or Moore, instead of a Rubin. Heck, I could have even gotten away with being a Narbstrom, because Charles Narbstrom got to be in her group. Instead, I got paired up with George Paterson, Reese Pilth, Teddy Simone, and Jessica Serino. And Jessica is nothing in comparison to Katie. I shouldn't be talking, but if *I* don't even find a girl attractive, then that has to say something.

But with bad luck comes good luck at least: Katie's station is right next to ours. So if she ever has to borrow a pot or flour, she can always come to us. I might even get to be the one to hand it to her.

Until tomorrow . . .

~Peter

September 8, 20--
Friday

What I guessed would happen, happened. Steve Jones sat on the west side of the cafeteria today. Jordan, Casey, and Gary weren't with him—I guess because I'm lucky enough that they have lunch another period—but he had two new recruits with him. One of them was Tim Ridger, and the other was this kid I had French with last year. I think his name is Chris Christianson, but I'm not positive. I didn't think that Steve hung out with them, but I guess I was wrong because there they were, in plain sight, sitting at the corner table, glaring at Tommy Boots and me. Steve mouthed something to Tim, and they all began to laugh.

Halfway through the period, a juice carton soared through the air and struck the wall behind our table. I got sprayed, along with my math work—which I had to re-do—and Tommy Boots. Tommy Boots stood up, seeming pissed, but sat back down when I asked him to. I'm not sure if he really would have done anything or not—he is more outgoing than me—but I didn't want him to take any chances. The Clan already has it out for John, and if both of my friends disappeared, then what would I do?

The flight of the juice box was followed by violent mocking. That kid, Chris, kept shouting out: *"Juicy juice, juicy juice, baby's got his juicy juice!"* while he pointed a finger, and the rest of the cafeteria laughed. The lunch aide who sat on duty, and whose job it was to watch that nothing like that happened, wasn't at her post—she was probably in the bathroom due to the chili burgers the cafeteria was serving—and Steve and them got away with it. I swear, one day they're going to go too far and get what's coming to them. I really hope someone puts them in their place.

That was lunch. In English, Jordan whispered, *"Juicy juice"* in my ear throughout the duration of the period. Apparently Steve had met up with him in the hall and told him about his most recent assault. I ignored him, barely being able to concentrate on *Othello.* Sometimes I think Jordan resembles Iago, the cunning backstabber, and my group of friends are more like Cassio.

That was pretty much my day at school, nothing out of the ordinary happened after that. John and I talked in Mr. Cane's class, while he droned on and on about the reproductive organs, and in Home Ec. I watched Katie skirt the room in her new blue skirt.

When I got home, I re-did my math and finished the rest of my homework and went over Tommy Boots's house with John. There, we talked about Jordan Saunders and what we would love to do to him and the rest of The Clan. Do they rent out hired thugs? I wish they did because we would hire some.

For dinner, I had grilled chicken and mashed potatoes, and my parents asked me how school was going. I lied, of course, and said that it was going great and asked if they could pass more mashed potatoes. We talked for the remainder of the dinner hour until they went to bed. Maybe it's just me, but now that I think about it, they seemed more talkative!

~Peter

September 9, 20--
Saturday

All right, Saturday! Yeeha!

I'm extremely happy it's the weekend, if you couldn't tell. The first weekend of school!

After dinner and writing in my journal last night, I went back over Tommy Boots's house. John returned as well, and we played the *Witch Hunter* card game and WOW. I swear that game is amazing. If I could be a Tauren or an Undead Warlock, I think life would be a lot cooler. If that was the case, then The Clan couldn't bother any of us, we'd just use our mana or eat them. That was pretty much the remainder of the night: after WOW, we watched a few episodes of *Witch Hunter* on DVD and went to sleep.

Today John's mom drove us out to the Bayview Mall again. There, we pretty much roamed around aimlessly scoping out computer games in Game Stop and looking at books in Borders. I used my gift card and bought two books: *18 Best Stories* by Edgar Allen Poe, and the other: *Lord of the Flies*. There's something about a fantasy world that soothes me, and since I've started reading again, nothing can placate the hardships of school like getting lost in a good book (that or writing in my journal).

While we were in the food court, I brought up Jordan

Saunders to John and asked him if he was scared. He said no, but I knew he was lying. When a member of The Clan has it out for you, you will be one scared puppy. It isn't like having them pick on you, because in some aberrant way, that really isn't getting beaten up. Somehow—I can only imagine—what they would do to John would be ten times worse.

After the mall, John's mom took us out to McDonald's, where we had a late lunch. I got a regular burger—hold the cheese, I'm trying to lose weight—and a medium strawberry shake. From there, she dropped each of us off at our houses, and this is where time elapses to and I'm writing this entry.

Later tonight, John and Tommy Boots will be coming over for a sleepover. My computer setup isn't as cool as Tommy Boots's, but it'll do to play a few games on. And if all else fails, we can play *Perfect Dark* on Xbox 360.

I'll write again tomorrow.

~Peter

September 10, 20--
Sunday

The remainder of last night was fun. We pretty much stayed up the whole night, swapping between *Perfect Dark* and *Halo 3*.

They left at two-thirty p.m. today, which was about two hours after we woke up for breakfast, or, due to the hour, lunch. Corolla made us bacon and eggs and slipped some cheese in for John. He likes his eggs omelet-style.

Now, here's the best part: after they left and my parents and I went to church, my dad talked to me, *actually* spent the remainder of the day with me. Since Sunday is the only day he and my mom have off, he's usually spending it with her or finishing up some project of his. Not today though. My mom had asked him to clean the gutters, and he said he was taking me to the park to have a catch instead. It's funny because when I heard him say it from downstairs, I had no idea who he meant, but when he knocked on my door and threw a glove on my lap, the light bulb above my head exploded in understanding. I erupted in elation, stuck the glove on my hand, and ran down the stairs to the garage.

We played in the park for about two hours. It was actually amazing: me in the park, not having a care in the world if Steve Jones or Jordan Saunders saw me. I knew my dad would protect me. It was great!

I wish every Sunday could be like this. (I'd choose baseball over fishing any day!)

While playing I got my dad to talk about his job, Grandma and Grandpa, and on his own, he even brought up his brother Tom (Uncle Tom), Aunt Megan, and their kids (my other cousins). He said that maybe next Sunday just me and him could take a ride out there and spend the day with them. *"Just us guys,"* he had said, *"taking a trip to visit your cousins."* I told him I'd be more than happy to.

That was my day.

Next Sunday is going to be great! Until then, let's see how this week unfolds. Hopefully, if things are going the way they seem to be, it'll turn out good. Maybe I'll even talk to Katie.

~Peter

September 11, 20--
Monday

Today was a sad day. Not for me, but for everyone who lost their loved ones in 2001.

Dr. Otto, our principal, broadcasted over the homeroom announcements that there would be a memorial service for an hour held after first period, and that the remaining periods would be shortened seven minutes to accommodate for the service. One kid was absent in my class, David White, and I'm guessing it was due to what day it was.

Outside, by the flagpole, the faculty had set up chairs for themselves in two vertical rows, and as they led their students onto the patch of grass, they had them sit between them. At the front of this stood a podium. Dr. Otto stood there greeting the teachers and students as they arrived, and about five minutes after everyone had sat down—teachers in chairs, students sitting cross-legged on the grass—he began his speech.

He mentioned how on this particular day a group of terrorists hijacked airliners and crashed two of them into the twin towers in New York City. He also stated that our finest—the FDNY—risked their lives to put out the fire and vacate anybody who had been hurt or trapped in the buildings as they crumbled amongst them, trapping them inside. He said that these people were heroes who risked their lives for the lives of others and that we could learn a great deal from them. He said that he sympathizes for those of us who have lost any loved ones on that tragic day back in 2001, and that those lost will not be forgotten.

This went on for about forty-five minutes until he concluded his speech by saying that each student who wished to lay a rose down by the flagpole and say a prayer for a lost one was more than welcome to. He had one of the janitors bring out a bushel of single roses in one of those wheelie carts and stand it by the podium. When he was done talking at least a hundred students and a bunch of the faculty came up to lay down a rose.

During this, I saw Gary Reith place one by the flagpole. I had no idea then, but as the day progressed, I learned—overheard actually—from Paul Rubkes that Gary had lost his father on that day. Maybe Gary isn't that much of a bad kid; maybe he's just looking for an outlet for his grief.

Nothing more happened today that I want to write about. Everyone was pretty much grief stricken, and every class talked about 9/11.

Thank God my parents' buildings are on the opposite side of Manhattan. I don't know what I would do without them.

~Peter

September 12, 20--
Tuesday

She's my partner!

She's my partner!

Katie Murgelsy is my partner!

Ha ha!!!! I'm going crazy.

I hope we get married!

I know yesterday was a morbid day for a lot of people, but today changes everything. From bad hatches good, I guess, as I had said earlier, or something like that anyway. Let me tell you all about this!!!

It happened in Mrs. Rugerrielli's class. Remember I mentioned earlier how we all had to do that reading from the French book? And how I wished I could have been Beau, Adora's husband? Well this is just as good, even better. Mrs. Rugerrielli assigned us partners to do a verbal interaction. We had to put our names in Henry Rodgers's hat and pick. Katie picked my name! I know it wasn't intentional, and there would have been no way for her to know which piece of paper was mine, but she picked me just the same, and I'm as happy as can be!

This afforded me the opportunity to talk to her for the majority of the class. We had to decide what type of situation we found ourselves in (in a car ride, having breakfast, out to the movies; that sort of thing), and what we would say to one another during our interaction.

Never had I thought a voice sounded more lovely than hers.

She wore another halter top: this one pink with white horizontal stripes and pink straps along with pink ~~capries~~ ~~capres~~ caprees (I give up on the spelling) that were really snug fitting. She got up once to go to the bathroom while I pondered about our situation, and I couldn't help but stare. When she came back, I told her the ones I came up with, and she agreed on the date to the movies. At the time, I had told myself that coming up with the lines would be very easy, all I had to do was picture it as a real date! But it proved to be more trying than I thought.

We got halfway through our dialogue when the bell rang, and she said that maybe we'd have time to finish before Home Ec. If not, then tomorrow.

Sweet Katie.

It turned out that she was late to Home Ec., and we couldn't work on it, so tomorrow is the day!

I'm so happy!

I'll be having good dreams tonight.

~Peter

September 13, 20--
Wednesday

I didn't really write about it last night, but over dinner both my mom and dad continued to be loquacious. They asked me about school again and about all my classes. Like last year, I fed them the answers they wanted to hear. The only lie I didn't make, besides my good grades, was about the teachers. I said that I found them really fun as well. It's true; if it wasn't for Mrs. Rugerrielli's verbal interaction assignment then I would have never talked to Katie at all (I hope this segues into us talking in Home Ec). Which reminds me, I just got done translating the last of my dialogue for our verbal interaction project. *Phew!*

In Home Ec. Katie came in early, and we finished deciding what to say to each other in English. Mrs. Rugerrielli didn't allot any more time for this in her class since we had to go on with the unit, so Home Ec. seemed like the most logical choice. I think it might have been possible for me to ask Katie for her number or screen name during this time, but I'm way too chicken and was not up to that. Plus, I don't think I could take the possible rejection. Tonight, Katie and I were supposed to translate our lines and study them. Mrs. Rugerrielli said that tomorrow she is going to give us some time to rehearse before our graded interaction on Friday. I'm sure we'll do great; I already memorized half my lines. It's just up to Katie to study hers.

That's all the new news with Katie and me, nothing more to tell until it happens. In English, Jordan Saunders poked me again and called me Pony-boy, then whispered that John would get his soon. I sympathized how this kid's friend's father had died and how all of them can go on acting the way they do. I don't understand bullies, maybe I never will.

At lunch, Steve and his new friends, Chris and Tim, started by throwing parts of their soft pretzels at Tommy Boots and me when the aide wasn't looking. I debated on telling on them and decided not to. If she didn't believe me, then I'd just get picked on more. I'd rather take the hit. That's at least what I told Tommy Boots. He just sighed and put his head down. I think Steve might have been putting rock salt in a straw and shooting it at me like a spitball because something small and hard stung my ear.

I hate them.

And this wasn't the end of it for today, either. I forgot to write that in Gym class—we're doing volleyball now and have already gotten into the lesson portion of bumping and setting—Steve hurled a volleyball under the net into my stomach. It hurt, and I almost threw up. Also, in Health, Mr. Cane turned his back to put on a video about the reproductive system, and when he did, Gary Reith threw a paper airplane into my head. I looked at it, and it had a message to John. I guess they wanted to kill two birds with one stone—hitting me and letting me deliver it to John. The message was about Jordan Saunders being pissed.

That was all though, just a lot of barking and no biting. We'll see if anything happens tomorrow.

I hope nothing does.

And now, finally, onto something good to close this entry. At dinner, my parents still expressed their garrulousness. I really think things are going to pull through for them.

Things are really looking up: my parents seem to be talking more, and now I'm talking to Katie Murgelsy! Hey, if The Clan stopped bothering me, then life would be at its vertex!

~Peter

September 14, 20--
Thursday

Today, Katie and I got to rehearse our lines. She's not quite up to par with her French as I am, and I had to help her out a little. It almost reminded me of my dad's situation, except in reverse. Which brings me to dinner.

My parents asked a lot about school tonight. I mean *a lot!* more than normal. It wasn't general like "how was school today?" It was more along the lines of, "So, Peter, how are things going in Mr. Cane's class? What are you learning about?" Stuff like that. My mom even tried to hone in on the specifics of my dealings with the students by asking if John and I talked a lot in Mr. Clemmings's class. When did she ever ask if John and I talked during class? This brings me to believe that they know something that I don't, that maybe one of the teachers sent a note home about my behavior (even though I don't see what they could possibly complain about), or worse—other student's behavior towards me. I don't play the role of the pacifist just because I know I'll get my rear end handed to me if I didn't. I also do it for the reason that I don't want to arouse suspicion and have a letter sent home because a teacher is concerned about me. What do you think would happen if my parents found out that my whole school career was one big joke and that their "beloved" son, their "well-liked" son, was really just a laughing stock that got picked on every day? My world would crumble at home as well as at school, that's what would happen.

But I'm probably just getting my heart rate up for nothing; maybe my parents *are* truly interested. If the school in fact had sent a letter home, I surely would have seen it before my parents did, right? And if that was the case, I would have destroyed it. Corolla puts the mail in the same spot she always does, and I constantly check it every day before my parents come home, and I've never found a letter before. So, I guess I'm making a big fuss out of nothing. I guess I should just accept the fact that maybe my parents are becoming genuinely interested in what I do now.

I just thought that day would never come, that's all. God surprises us in many ways. Praise all the good in this world! Praise God. Amen.

On another good note, Steve was absent today, and lunch was a smooth sail. Steve's new disciples didn't think to do anything without him, although seeing him absent did cause a ball of apprehension to become lodged in my throat: it made me think about what would happen if Tommy Boots was absent. Sure Steve wouldn't do anything entirely harsh with the both of us sitting together, but what if it was just me?

I shudder to think.

Next topic: Home Ec.

George Paterson, Jessica Serino, Reese Pilth, Teddy Simone, and I learned how to bake cakes today. My secret hope didn't come true, though. Katie didn't come over and ask for eggs or flour, but I did get to watch as she bent over to find the cake tin. She's beautiful.

Update on the whole mess with John and The Clan: nothing is FUBAR. Actually, nothing has even happened. Maybe the whole thing was just a red herring meant to drive us crazy in anticipation. Who knows?

All that I know is that tomorrow is my verbal interaction with Katie, and I'm kind of nervous. I got my lines down now, but she needed a lot of help. I just hope she can pull through. I can't have my grades slip; they are the one thing I can show for myself.

~Peter

September 15, 20--
Friday

I can't sleep so I figured I'd write instead.

It's five a.m., but I woke up at four and spent a half an hour with my dad at the breakfast table eating Cheerios. They're supposed to be good for your cholesterol; that's why he eats them, and since I'm his son and high cholesterol is hereditary, I probably should start eating them daily as well if I want to nip this thing in the bud.

My dad asked what I had going on in school today, and I told him about my verbal interaction. I left out Katie's name. I don't want him to think I like a girl or anything. I don't know what I'd do if he tried to give me advice. The last advice with Corolla completely backfired, plus he might say something mushy, and it might make me think about that all day instead of the verbal.

He said that he had to go to the Marriott today for some conference. I don't really know what a computer stock analyst does, but he said that his company, C.V.C. Innovations, has to give a presentation to some bigger company, and they need him to speak about the numbers. It's always about the numbers with my dad's life. If the numbers are good, things must be good as well. *"It's a direct correlation,"* he says. Those are his thoughts on my school experience as well: if I have good grades, then I must be doing well and having a good time. Up until the other day, with Katie becoming my partner, that logic was completely false.

After talking with my dad, I came back here, in my room, and looked over my verbal dialogue again. I know it backwards and forwards, in and out, in English and in French. If Katie can pull through, I think we can get an A+ on it. And I think she can, too. She's a smart girl.

I would love for her to be my girlfriend.

Wish me luck, and I'll write tomorrow to let you know how all this went.

~Peter

September 15, 20--
Entry 2

I CAN'T BELIEVE THIS!

I HATE my parents! I ABHOR school! I LOATHE life!

I hate to reopen my entry from this morning, but I have to get my feelings out OR ELSE I'M GOING TO EXPLODE!!!!!

My parents just told me over dinner—OVER DINNER!!! THE ONE SOLACE OF MY DAY WITH THEM—that they are going to get a DIVORCE!

I knew they were having problems, but I thought they were working them out and that the little spiel on the fourth had set them straight for a revival of their romance. I guess I was wrong—wrong with everything.

I HATE LIFE!!!!!!!!!!!!!!!!!!!

This ruins everything. I don't even know how to write about this. Now what do I have to look forward to? I thought that maybe, one day, I would meet someone and end up happily married like my parents had . . . *had*. But now I don't even know if marrying *anyone* is a possibility.

If *my own* parents can't stay together, then what makes me think that a lummox like myself will be able to? I won't, that's just the thing. If I could even possibly, somehow manage to land a girl that would want to go out with me, let alone get married, she'd divorce me for sure—as I'm being taught by the wonderful example of my parents—and I'd kill myself (not literally, that would be a wrongful sin, and I'd never do it, which traps me even further in living a life not worth living).

It all makes sense now. I can see it all happening. And if we have kids like me? God, help them.

That's another thing . . . if God is so omniscient, omnipotent, and benevolent, then why would He let something like this happen? I don't want to start sounding needy, but why me? I honestly think I deserve an answer to that question: WHY ME? I pray to God EVERY night—I'm even capitalizing His name and the possessive form of "he" when I write about Him—and have endured countless beatings throughout my life by kids who curse His very name in vain and in sacrilege (something of which I have never done) and this is the thanks I get? *If* He really does exist

(. . . IF . . .)

then I'm really beginning to question His goodness and His plan for my life. If this is how He is going to treat someone who follows and worships His guidance, then I just might begin to worship someone else.

God, please give me strength to get through this. I don't ask for much and you know this. Please, please, PLEASE! Give me the strength to get through this.

~Peter

September 16, 20--
Saturday

It's Saturday, and I spent the whole day in my room. I only came out to eat—the little food that I can stand to hold down—and go to the bathroom. About noon, Corolla knocked on my door and asked if I was all right. I told her I wasn't feeling well and just wanted to lie down. I don't think my parents told her the news. And why should they? Corolla wasn't really a part of our family, only a maid who cooks for me, cleans the house, and more or less raised me! I don't know if I'm mad or glad that they didn't tell her, but I'm going to keep my mouth shut and leave it up to them to tell her. I guess eventually she'll find out like the rest of the world.

I only hope that the kids at school don't find out. It would just be more gasoline for their fire. I would think Gary Reith, of all people, would understand, considering how his father died, but somehow I don't think he would at all. Kids like him just like to cause others pain to feel good about themselves.

I honestly can't believe they're getting a divorce. It still hasn't really sunk in. And of all days to tell me, they had to tell me on a Friday, completely ruining my weekend. Tommy Boots, John, and I had planned to go out to Bayview again, but nope, not when poor old Peter is constantly throwing up in the toilet. Who would want a kid like that tagging along?

I haven't told them yet. I just said I wasn't feeling well and that I'd see them on Monday in school. I guess they had the sleepover without me.

Better off that way.

I don't feel like writing. Maybe I'll write tomorrow. We'll see.

~Peter

P.S. Shoot me. End my pain.

September 17, 20--
Sunday

You want to know how to make a bad situation worse? Add school to it. I'm obviously not over the breaking news—and probably never will be—and now I have to go to school tomorrow? I can't even remember, but I think Mrs. Foxwood is giving us an in-class essay. How am I going to write?

My parents should be home today, since it's Sunday, but I haven't seen them. They didn't call me down for church, and I wound up missing it. I hope God doesn't get upset with me.

I don't think I can stand to see my parents yet, anyway, without feeling that sickness creep back into my stomach, summoning me to spill my lunch. Dinner tonight will consist of the Ritz crackers I stowed in my closet from yesterday. They seem to hold.

I heard the garage door opening at eight this morning, and I don't even think my dad's home. He probably went fishing or to my cousins' without me to get away from my mom. It makes sense now why he told me it would be "just us guys" visiting them. It also means that he knew about the divorce and didn't tell me. I doubt him and Mom will be spending any time together now that this whole mess is out in the open. I still can't believe they told me they still loved me and that they don't want this decision to affect the way I view them. Were they kidding? How could this *not* affect that?

I just started this entry and already I'm finding myself sick to my stomach. I guess I can't express my feelings right now. I'm sorry. I can only imagine what joys tomorrow will bring.

~Peter

September 18, 20--
Monday

As if things couldn't get any worse.

Today The Clan finally got their revenge on John. They jumped him right after Social Studies. I tried to stop them, but Casey Vector punched me in the stomach, which sent me to the floor, cowering in agony. Why doesn't God answer my prayers?

It happened like this . . . wait, let me start at first period, when Gary Reith eyed me from across the room. Mr. Rugerdy was instructing us to get out our graphing calculators, so we could start on the lesson of binomial integers and parabolas, when Beth Kilterly passed me a note. At first I didn't know what to think; I was in total awe. Then, when she motioned to me that it was from Gary, it pretty much hit me—she'd never pass me a note unless someone popular told her to.

The note was simple. It looked like this:

today is the day poneyboy

be ready...

I thought it was very ambiguous at the time but that proved to be wrong soon enough.

Of course I told both John and Tommy Boots about it next period in Chem., but they said The Clan was probably just starting stuff like they always did, and I had to agree with them. It seemed like their style.

All that changed in fourth period. Mr. Clemmings ended the day's lesson on World War II and dismissed the class, retiring to his second desk in the back corner of the room. While we were walking out and Mr. Clemmings was distracted, Steve Jones came from behind and twisted my arm behind my back, forcing me out into the hall, which by then was mobbed with chattering students. Casey grabbed John, and The Clan led us both into the boy's bathroom across the hall. It's safe to say I'm never going to the bathroom in school again, not now that I know what can happen in there. I tried to scream, but my voice was lost in the jubilant chatter of kids. The sound of it echoing throughout the bathroom will haunt me for years to come.

That's when Jordan Saunders kicked John in the testicles as Casey held him. John let out a bloodcurdling shriek of pain and collapsed to the ground. I tried to struggle free but couldn't and decided to spit on Casey. I honestly don't know what made me do it. I think it was the surge of adrenaline at seeing one of my best friends getting hurt. Whatever it was, it turned out to be a big mistake because he came over to me and landed a swift punch in my jelly-gut, sending me to my knees. I felt the air escape my lungs and my trachea close off and the bile in my stomach wanting to dance up my throat. I held it down somehow and managed to catch my breath.

As I was doing this, I was helpless to watch as the three of them punched, kicked, and slapped John. They made it a point to stay away from his face for some reason, calling out: *"Put some ointment on those pimples and get rid of that crap!"* But just the same, he took the beating of his life. The Clan swore that if he or I told on them, then they would do this to him and me every day for the rest of our lives. As far as I know, John didn't say anything. I sure know I didn't.

Since I had lunch next period, I decided to stay in the bathroom with John while he cut Math and tried to recover. He told me to go down and bring Tommy Boots back up. I did. There, the three of us sat: John writhing and shaking from pain, and me clutching at my bruised stomach, as we both told Tommy Boots what had happened.

As I said before: *As if things couldn't get any worse.*

That was my trouble at school, and it's safe to say that I probably failed Mrs. Foxwood's in-class essay the period after with flying colors. My mind just wouldn't work, and I couldn't think of English. All I could think about was seeing Jordan Saunders's fist crash into John's stomach and that twisted malevolent grin on his face as he did it. That, and my parents' divorce.

God, I pray that you will hear my prayer and subject The Clan to a penalty for the offense of beating John and me up.

On top of all this, I now realize why my parents have become so talkative with me at dinner—which I decided to try eating at the table tonight. The pain in my stomach had subsided by then, and I guess I had lived with the sick knowledge of the soon-to-be divorce long enough to start eating their food again. The reason they were talking to me so much was so they didn't have to talk to *each other* and possibly to try to gain a vantage point over one another with my love.

God, I feel so used.

The moment I realized this, I excused myself and "went to bed early," claiming I was tired from a long day at school. If only they knew my trials. If they only knew. And God, they used me . . . they used me . . . LIKE SOME KIND OF STUPID PIECE IN A CHESS GAME!!!

I HATE THEM!

~Peter

September 19, 20--
Tuesday

John seemed a little better today. He said he's got black-and-blues over the thoracic part of his body, and when he showed them to Tommy Boots and me, I noticed that they had taken on the yellowish tint that soon follows after. It was pretty bad. Thankfully it wasn't noticeable. Thinking back, maybe that's why The Clan had focused on his body reign only—the face would surely show the harsh trial he had been through.

In English Jordan poked me in the back and whispered, *"Hey, Pony-boy, your boyfriend feeling all right? Hope I didn't hurt him* too *bad.*" He's a jerk, and after he said that, I peered over toward Casey, who, in return, gave a wicked sneer. They were happy with what they had done. Probably even more happy that they had gotten away with it, as well. I need guidance; I really don't know what to do anymore about them. Oh yeah, I almost forgot, Jordan also kept whispering "Dough-boy" throughout that class as well. Probably because my stomach almost swallowed Casey Vector's fist when he plunged it into me.

Gym wasn't much better either. Tommy Boots, John, and I had to deal with Steve, who kept aiming the volleyballs towards us when he hit them. One of them made contact with Tommy Boots's head and almost sent him sprawling to the ground. It was more of a shock really than anything; they're not hard. But it's the principle of the matter.

I guess I should write about something more positive rather than all these negative points but it's really hard when there is an enormous outpouring of it. I'll try anyway. In French, Katie hasn't really talked to me since our verbal interaction assignment. Did I ever mention how we did on that by the way? Hold on let me check . . .

No, I didn't, and it makes sense why (I wish not to reiterate). We received an eighty-eight, which, when translated in letter grades, amounts to a B+. Not bad, but not great either. I'm used to getting As. I don't like to place blame on others who seem good-hearted, but Katie kind of messed up. She stumbled on the part about buying popcorn and I had to whisper the right words in her ear. Mrs. Rugerrielli heard me and said, *"No fair helping, Peter."* She's a good teacher, and didn't take off any points for that, just for the long pauses and the constant "uhhhs" and "ummms" by Katie. And since it was a group project I had to share the grade.

That was then and this is now. And now she's reverted back to the way she was when we first started this year: not talking to me. I'm not sure if she got word of my reputation or if I didn't try hard enough to attain a friendship while I had the chance. Like I said: it's really hard for me to talk to girls, and I guess I gave it my best shot. I can't really see myself striking up a conversation with her now; it'd be too awkward, like trying to rekindle a fire in the rain. But maybe we'll get paired up again for a project in the future. We'll just have to see what the upcoming days have to bring.

Looking back on the blurb I just wrote, I realize I did the antithesis of what I had intended on doing: writing something positive rather than something somewhat negative. Can you blame me though? I don't think I have anything positive in my life going on right now. Which brings me to dinner . . .

My parents continued to talk to me separately, but I knew it was only to punish the other to dwell in silence. That silence was maddening, and I felt their pain. Nothing is worse than knowing that you're the cause of your parents' pain, even if it's indirect. I remained at the table for the full hour tonight and ate the majority of the food on my plate—after a few days of only nibbling rations you do get sort of hungry. I think I learned everything there is about investment banking and a lot more than I wanted to know about computer analyzation. Is that even a real word? Analyzation? Who cares? It's as if my parents are using me as their psychologist, which brings me to the major topic over dinner; I guess I'm already repressing the idea of it. My parents want to hire a psychologist for me so that I can "properly cope" with their divorce. A person to hold my hand if you will—someone other than themselves.

I think the idea is stupid. I don't trust psychologists, and I don't want another person prying their way into my private life. They're probably going to ask questions about school and somehow get it out of me that I get picked on, and then tell my parents. If they found out, they'd tell the school, and the school would expel The Clan, and then if they saw me outside of school, or whenever they were let back in, I'd be a dead man. No, I don't want a psychologist. They're nothing but trouble and can't lead to anything positive. This journal right here is the perfect doctor to listen to my problems. It can't make negative comments and try to analyze me. It can't question me, and it *can* keep a secret. It lets me pour out my thoughts and I feel better.

Please Mom and Dad, no psychologist.

Please . . .

~Peter

September 20, 20--
Wednesday

Gary Reith started with me in Math today. I think the nickname "Pony-boy" has transmogrified into "Dough-boy" now because he kept mouthing it from across the room. What does he get out of it but a tired mouth? I guess a lot, because it really does bother me. Kudos to you Gary, you jerk. Kudos. I pretty much found myself lost in class after that. My mind kept bringing up his face mouthing those words, and every time I seemed to turn my head in his direction, he was still doing it. I hope it results in him failing. Maintaining a passing grade in AP Math isn't that easy. Just the same, I hope I don't falter in my own grades.

John seemed much better when I saw him and Tommy Boots next period in Chemistry. And since we didn't have Gym, it was a Clan-free two periods. My head was still in the clouds, and I couldn't pay attention to Mrs. Pastorelli. Tommy Boots gave me his notes at lunch, and I copied them so I really didn't miss a great deal except for her demonstration on the effects of pure sodium in water. I seem to remember a distant blur of fire, but not entirely. Tommy Boots backed up my blurred reality by saying that's indeed what it was: a controlled environment where Mrs. Pastorelli dropped a small tablet of sodium into a beaker. Like I said: I didn't miss a great deal of anything. When would that type of information ever become useful? Which brings me to think about half the other un-useful information we learn at school. Imaginary numbers? Integers? Graphing binomial equations? Unless I'm going to be a professional in that particular field, I'll probably never use it. I don't even know why I'm thinking like this, I guess it's the idea of the divorce plaguing my mind, staining it with its begrimed iniquity.

Now that I think about it, I should start writing these entries in a good/bad partition. Maybe that will force me to focus on the good aspects more, rather then meshing them in with the bad.

Okay here it goes:

Good: English.

Despite the fact that I thought I did horrible on Mrs. Foxwood's English essay, I was wrong. I got an A+. That's always good, and it goes to show you that sometimes, even though you think the world may be against you, you can still produce something positive out of a negative.

Good: Home Ec.

My long dreams of Katie Murgelsy coming over and asking to borrow flour finally came true. Even though she asked Teddy Simone instead of me, I still got a smile out of it. Maybe she'll start talking to me now. I hope so. I really need more good things to happen.

Good: Lunch.

Steve and his new goons weren't present on our side of the cafeteria. Even though I saw them on the east wing, they didn't come over to the west. I guess they were too busy doing whatever they were doing (I did see a few girls scattered about their table so I guess that's why). Thankfully Katie wasn't amongst any of them. My dreams just might be crushed if she took a dive to the dark side.

And to top it all off, Corolla packed me not one, but two peanut butter and jelly sandwiches with a note that said:

You look like

Sorry, I thought I heard someone coming into my room, but it was probably just my mom or dad walking into theirs. Okay, the note said:

You look like lose peso

Comer! Grow!

—Corolla

I guess she still thinks kids have to be overly plump to be healthy, but whatever, I took that extra sandwich with great gratitude. It made everything feel just right.

Now on to the bad.

Bad: Health.

Mr. Cane had his head in the clouds and his back to the class most of the time, which enabled Steve to fly another paper airplane at me. This time into the side of my face, thankfully missing my eye. The note scribbled on it was once again for John. It said:

yous better keep youre mouth shut

or thats the next part of you we punch!

It was harsh, straight to the point, and grammatically incorrect. I doubt John will be telling on them, but them sending a note this way signifies that they're scared, and when you back a dog into a corner, it usually starts to bite.

Bad: Social Studies.

Jordan kept mimicking punching himself upside the head. I guess it was aimed at John, but I caught the majority of this. Needless to say, I spent the whole period in trepidation of being hauled out into the boy's room again. Thankfully it didn't happen, but sometimes it's the fear that's instilled that gets you more than the actions.

I'm still feeling down. I think I should have reversed the order in which I wrote, starting with the bad and transitioning to the good. I'll have to do that for next time but for now I'm going to go back and read the good parts again to counter this negative feeling I've summoned.

~Peter

September 20, 20--
Entry 2

You've probably already figured out that by me reopening an entry it means some horrible deed has unfolded. And it has. Since I only ate half my dinner tonight due to that argument my . . . did I even write that?

No, I didn't, sorry. To make a long story short, over dinner, my mom and dad were still battling one another subconsciously, and I guess that during one of my dad's spiels about work, my mom got so fed up about it she started yelling and shouting at him. I wanted to have nothing to do with this, ~~and by~~ so I ran up to my room, saying I was full. And since I had only eaten half my dinner, I woke up in the middle of the night, starving. That's when I went downstairs to get something out of the fridge and saw the most horrible sight I would ever think to see in my house . . .

It's not anything like one of my parents being murdered and sprawled out, marinating in a pool of their own blood or anything like that. But it was still horrible. It was my dad sleeping on the couch downstairs. And seeing this broke my heart.

I had no idea they weren't sleeping in the same room anymore. How long has this been going on? It made the idea of the divorce exceedingly concrete in my mind. It was

DEFINITELY going to happen. It wasn't like one of their earlier fights where they just said stuff to one another and made up afterwards. This one IS serious. And they ARE going to go through with it.

Why are they doing this? Don't they still love each other? Don't they love me? Was any of it my fault?

I thought that if I didn't say anything, and let them discuss it between themselves, then they would come to realize they're wrong and dismiss the whole stupid idea as nonsense and nothing more—an idea which I honestly had thought in the deepest depths of my heart to be no more than a maneuver to jounce the opposing party back on track. Now I know I was wrong. Now I know how serious this is. And it hurts. It hurts so damn bad. Like a serrated knife that can't be removed, twisting itself deeper into my heart. And the one who's plunging it further is this entity called divorce, and it is holding hands with my parents, smiling.

It's smiling . . .

~Peter

September 21, 20--
Thursday

I didn't feel like going to school today, especially after seeing what I saw last night. I barely even fell back asleep. Let me say that by the time I finally *did* fall asleep and woke up, my stomach was a twisting knot, gnawing at itself for food. Can the stomach actually eat itself? I'm not sure, but if it could, then mine may have already started this morning. I can only imagine what Gandhi must have gone through during his hunger strikes. Though I doubt Gandhi had that serrated knife lodged in his back to wound him further. I think I know more about pain than he does at this point—especially on that topic.

Even though I didn't feel like school, I had to go. If Corolla caught me at home then she would definitely know that I was cutting for some reason—something I never do. I guess I could have played sick but that would have meant that I would have to with that. She didn't even look at me. Oh well, it'd probably just end in a divorce anyway, just like my parents. At least Steve didn't know about it. I couldn't bear having him heckle me about that.

Now that I think about it, I don't think I ever mentioned the bus rides to and from school. It's not anything special, but I guess I should include them. Thankfully Jordan, Steve, Casey, or Gary are not on my route, and I don't have to deal with them in the morning or the afternoon. I don't think I'd be able to manage if they were. At least God (I'm warming back up to Him now; I guess He couldn't have prevented my parents' behavior and feelings) saw fit that my tormentors didn't have to live so close to me.

The seat I sit in is the fourth one from the front on the driver's side. Since I'm the fourth stop I pretty much get to pick my seat, and since I'm the fourth I think the fourth seat is rather clever. As for the left side, I like to think of it as evens and odds. If I associate the left side of the bus with odds and the right sides with evens then I can pick

September 22, 20--
Friday

Her name is Dr. Murgelsy. I kid you not. My parents had Corolla take me to her today after school and might I add what an awesome place to go on a Friday! (If you can't read my sarcasm please note that it is fully intended.)

I'm not positive that she's Katie's mom, and there's no way for certain to be sure unless I do a little detective work, but what kind of a coincidence is that? I felt like punching her in the face because of what she represents (my parents' divorce), and yet I felt sort of at ease because in some way she might be related to Katie. She seems nice enough. She's either in her late '40s or early '50s and has chestnut brown hair, a shade very close to Katie's. Every time I looked at her, Katie's face popped up in my mind.

Before I get off track I want to mention that I've decided that I'm not going to discuss anything school-related with this woman—under no circumstances will that happen. As I've mentioned in previous entries: it could lead to a disaster. Instead, I'll just go along with what she has to say, maybe listen and nod in the right places, but never really take her advice. If she wants me to talk to her about my parents I guess I can't lie, but it'll never be the full truth either. How am I to trust a complete stranger with that type of information as well as my feelings? If you think about it, it's stupid. I honestly don't see how people can go to these types of people—psychologists—and just pour their hearts out.

I guess in order to fully understand what I felt walking into that office, I have to start from the top, so here I go, grit your teeth (or spiral spine) and bear with me . . .

The trip there wasn't that long—it took us fifteen minutes since its only over on Cranberry Avenue, and Corolla, driving me in her red Toyota Corolla, played Spanish music the whole way there. (Sometimes I wonder if she got her car by accident, telling the dealer her name and him confusing it for the model he thought she wanted.) When we arrived, she asked me if I was nervous. I told her that I wasn't. I lied. I think the music somehow augmented my fears of what to expect.

When we got to the big white stucco building, building 154, I slumped out of the seat and began walking beside Corolla towards the doors. It was like a death walk one might amble down the Green Mile. I never even got my last meal.

Corolla opened the door for me, and I stepped in reluctantly enough.

Dr. Murgelsy's office was on the second floor, room 253, but at the time I didn't know that, because if I had, then my total shock wouldn't have been very surprising. Corolla knew the name of the doctor, but since I'd never asked, she never mentioned it. The only thing we ended up doing when we walked through the tinted doors was walk up to one of those information panels where the lists of names are posted. I wasn't in my most observant mood, so instead of reading it, I just looked at the multitude of plants residing in the pebbled sea, which sat in the far off corner. Corolla lightly tapped my arm and told me in her best English that we had to go to the elevators. It came out, *"Peter ascensor, elevatored, elevatored, go up to office, 253."* I understood what she meant—that we'd have to dance with the devil in a suspended cage of death before meeting the imping psychologist. Living with her has enabled me to have a keen ear for broken English and her poor pronunciations. How else would I have understood her advice about that girl that one time? Thinking back, it would have been better if I hadn't understood her at all.

After stepping out of the elevator, we found suite 253, and I still didn't notice the nameplate; I was too distraught and looking at my feet, trying to bring my mind elsewhere like a protesting, flame-engulfed Buddhist monk, concentrating on his prayers or some soothing image of a Caribbean beach.

The wait was twenty minutes before my winning nomination, if you will, of walking up and accepting the award of the last sound day of my life. And when my name was finally called, I almost thought my heart stopped.

Peter Rubin, Dr. Murgelsy will see you now.

God, how those words thrummed in my head and played my brain like a drum set. It was unreal. And at that moment, I wasn't on Earth anymore. Instead, I found myself on a recurring rerun of an episode of *The Twilight Zone.*

That's when I met her, and as I described earlier, she was nice, and I had to abate my potential hate in the form of a long and silent sigh.

Once in her office, and after her greeting, Dr. Murgelsy—I'll never get used to either saying or writing that—went on to explain the situation as best as she knew it and asked me to fill in any details that she missed. She missed quite a few, but I said nothing. I think she did it on purpose, too, acting as a way to get me to open up.

Very conniving.

Being there also made me think of something else: when had my parents had the time to collaborate over hiring her? I hadn't really thought about that, but I guess they sucked it up on that account and did so they might pass the buck (me) onto her (Dr. Murgelsy). Maybe, in truth, they really feel that an officious person like this could do me good and they want to help me. But if that was the case, then why had they decided on the divorce in the first place? It's a catch twenty-two I guess.

Life sucks sometimes.

That was pretty much my meeting with Dr. Murgelsy. I learned that we would meet every Monday and Friday, and that each meeting would be an hour long. I learned that whatever I said to her would remain completely confidential. A good thing to know, but it doesn't change the fact that I'm not going to completely trust her. I also learned that her favorite color is purple, she likes dogs, and loves to read, like me. That was during our one-on-one discussion of "getting to know one another," as she put it. I kept mine simple, stating how I liked *Witch Hunter*, the mall, playing WOW, and hanging out with my friends (little does she know that I only have two). She didn't ask about them yet, but I know it's coming. Somehow, all that has some kind of underlying presence in her version of my parents' divorce. Watch, you'll see. In about two or three weeks I'll be writing, "I told you so!" in big block letters.

At least it's Friday, and the weekend is here. I almost forgot to mention that I'm writing this entry earlier than usual because I'm going to sleep over at Tommy Boots's house tonight with John. If I leave early enough, I won't have to see my parents and talk to them about my visit with Dr. Murgelsy. I'm sure they would have a hundred or so questions to ask me over dinner in their subconscious way of avoiding one another. I'm sure I'll be cornered into telling them sooner or later, but who says I can't put it off as long as I can?

As far as putting off telling Tommy Boots and John, I think I can do it adequately enough. Since I usually find myself at one of their houses on Friday after school, I'm sure questions will arise. I'll just attribute my lateness to homework. How long can I hide Dr. Murgelsy from them? I'm not sure. But I'm willing to find out.

~Peter

September 23, 20--
Saturday

It's about three in the afternoon, and I just got back from Tommy Boots's house. I'm home now because once again I want to try to avoid having to see or discuss anything with my parents. Maybe by me not being home it'll force them to engage in conversation with one another. I mean, they had to do it to hire Dr. Murgelsy, right? Maybe I can convince *them* to go see a psychologist or a marriage counselor to give them the jumpstart. Maybe that'd be the catalyst in rekindling their marriage.

All I know is that my dad's the one who comes home first on Saturdays since his company closes early today. With that being said I should probably hurry and finish writing this entry.

Last night was good. I arrived at Tommy Boots's house at about 5:30 p.m., an hour after Corolla and I got home from Dr. Murgelsy's office. When I got there, John was already assuming his position in one of the rocking video game chairs that Tommy Boots has. He has a total of two, and we have to rotate. We played the games he had and talked about the new and forthcoming *Witch Hunter* video game. It's reported to come out sometime this December, and I think the three of us will be the first of hundreds online at Game Stop in the

Bayview Mall to buy it.

Tonight I'll be sleeping over at John's house. I think next week they're going to look to sleep at mine, but I don't think that's a possibility with the impending divorce. What if one of them wakes up in the middle of the night and sees either my mom or dad sleeping on the couch like I did? I don't even know what they would think, and I don't want to have to subject them to that. More so, I don't want to put the inquisitive nature of my friends upon myself after seeing such a sight. I'm sure I'll figure out some excuse. Either way, tonight should be fun, and, like I said: It'll get me away from my parents for another day. I'm sure Sunday the both of them will be out of the house trying to avoid one another, my dad fishing and my mom doing God knows what she does.

:::Sigh:::

~Peter

September 24, 20--
Sunday

I thought that I dreaded school, but now it seems that it's sort of a safe haven for me. Only in regards to having an excuse of escaping my parents that is. Although if I look at the fact that they aren't even home during the time I go to school, then I can completely cancel out that logic.

I don't know, I'm just rambling on I guess. I really hate school and you know that. You've been with me through it all this year. And looking on the bright side, the first month of it is almost over.

Last night, as I had written, I went over John's house. We watched another really old movie called *Cast Away,* and I found it to be amazing. Truly an eye opener that touched my heart with invisible fingers. It was as if I was Chuck Noland. *I* had been the one cast away and abandoned on an uncharted island which was my house. Sure there were things that talked to me (my parents) the way Chuck Noland talked to Wilson in the movie, but were they really talking to me, or were they talking at me? I think I felt a little like that volleyball. Sure the movie made it seem like he loved the ball, and it was extremely emotional when he lost it (I hid a tear from both Tommy Boots and John at that one paramount moment), but wasn't he just using it as a device to keep himself from going completely batty? I think that was more so the case than him actually befriending it. The same case goes for my parents. I think I'm just there so they can use me to talk at, so they don't have to talk to one another or go crazy from the silence. It's a dismal analogy but I feel it fits my situation perfectly.

That was last night. Today I returned around four, putting off going home as late as possible, and when I arrived, neither my mom or my dad were around. It caused me to miss church but I knew my parents wouldn't be going anyway. I prayed in my room instead.

As if it were clockwork, both my parents came home at dinnertime and complained to one another how none was made. Did they really expect the other to have made it for them when they weren't home? Such trivialities are the driving factor of this divorce.

Needless to say, I "went to bed" early tonight to catch up on some "sleep." Right. It's here that I sit and write my feelings to you.

Tomorrow is yet another day in this merry-go-round of aggravation.

~Peter

September 25, 20--
Monday

It's Monday, which means that I went to see Dr. Murgelsy again.

It went okay, but this time there was no escaping my parents at dinner, and I pretty much fell prey to their questions about her. The first was from my dad, and it was if I liked her. I told him that it's really too soon to tell, but I think that she's nice. And that wasn't a lie—she really is nice. The remaining questions were from my mom, almost seeming to steal the spotlight from my dad. She pretty much asked what we talked about and this and that. I told her that Dr. Murgelsy said she's not allowed to disclose any of the information we talk about, and I feel the same way. I think that answer took my mom by surprise, but she nodded and continued to slurp her soup. I guess just the fact that I'm going to see a psychologist makes my parents feel better about having sprung the whole divorce thing in my face. But I'll tell you something: Dr. Murgelsy hasn't even talked about it yet.

On our first visit I was almost positive she was going to come right out and bring it up, but she hadn't. And on this visit she hadn't either; she just asked me more about *Witch Hunter* and WOW. She even had an Xbox 360 set up and played it with me. Let me just say that for an older woman, she isn't half bad. We played *Perfect Dark*, and she beat me three out of nine times. Not bad. I wonder how she'd be at Nerf Wars?

She never mentioned my parents once and never asked about school.

Now that I think of about it, when I was at Dr. Murgelsy's, I didn't even think about Katie, which is odd because she's been on my mind a lot lately; at school the idea of the two of them being related has been constantly gnawing at my cerebellum (especially in French and Home Ec). I felt that it would stick there all day like a piece of gum on the bottom of my shoe. But by the time I went to go see Dr. Murgelsy, I'd somehow forgotten about it. Maybe it was the way she talked to me or played video games, I'm not sure. Either way, the question is back now and it won't subside.

It's more than possible for two unrelated people to have the same last name. If you look in last year's yearbook, you'll see my picture next to Terry Rubin's, and I can assure you that we're not related at all.

Now that I think about it, I can't even look at Katie the same way anymore. During Mrs. Rugerrielli's class, I found myself staring at the back of her head, looking through her, thinking, trying to figure out if she's related to my psychologist or not. And what if she *is* Dr. Murgelsy's daughter? What would that mean? In reality, I don't think it would make any world of difference. Maybe I feel as if she'd spill the beans to her mother about me, but then again why would a person like her do such a thing? Unless, that is, she liked me, and I doubt that's the case. And if that ever did happen, what could her mother say? That my parents are going through a divorce and that she plays games with me? It's not something I should even worry about. What I should really be worrying about is Steve Jones.

Steve started with me today at lunch. He had his new disciples with him again, and they were sitting in the west wing. We had our usual table, Tommy Boots and I, and they were sitting directly across from us.

I think that his means of messages always come in the form of a flying object. Today, he sent a plane my way with another message scribbled on it. It was a drawing that looked like this:

It was crudely done, and I think that if Steve is taking Art this year (I'm not sure if he is or isn't), his teacher would be very disappointed in him. It doesn't matter though. I got the message clearly enough: They were going to focus their attention on me this time, now that John was "taken care of." I knew it would only be a matter of time.

Tommy Boots said that I should go see my guidance counselor or the principal, but that wouldn't work. If I did that and The Clan found out, I'd only be asking for a second beating on top of the first one: a two-for-one special, a sale on Peter Rubin, punches all around. I told him that I'd rather not say anything and see what happens. I've been taking beatings my whole life—rocks at the playground are the most vivid in my head (also literally)—and I guess I'm not afraid to take another. They're leaving John alone now, aren't they? If I let them get it out of their systems, I'm sure they'll leave me alone, too, and focus on some other shy, inward person before they start their cycle over again. And it'll be that in-between period where I'll have my sanctuary, my blissful harmony and absence of disturbance (from them at least—my mind, parents, and the divorce are completely different matters all together). But, in order to get to that period, I'll have to get through the present, and the present always comes with obstacles.

~Peter

September 26, 20--
Tuesday

I'm almost certain The Clan is going to let things play out for me the way they did with John: waiting for the most opportune moment, because none of them did anything to me today. I'm wrong. Sorry. Jordan *did* do something to me in Mrs. Foxwood's class, but I don't think it had any reference to the note Steve sent my way yesterday. I think Jordan took this one upon himself.

Since he sits behind me in English, I think he used his placement to his advantage and attacked me while my back was turned. He even did it mid-lesson without being caught. Maybe if I wasn't so overweight then Mrs. Foxwood could have seen what he was doing. But that's not the case is it? I guess I'd better stop beating around the bush and just write down what he did to me. Maybe that'll calm my nerves—it's amazing how you can still be wound up from something that happened over six hours ago.

Here's what he did . . . what I *think* he did at least. Remember, I had my back turned.

As Mrs. Foxwood was reading *The Raven* from her *English Now* textbook, I felt a white-hot, blinding pain on the back of my neck that can only be compared to the branding of a steer. It made me jump almost completely out of my seat and squall in surprise and detest of the pain. When I turned around to look at Jordan, he was just sitting in his seat nonchalantly, holding his pen as if he were taking notes. I think it was the pen that was his artillery. I think he rubbed the tip back and forth on the desk so fast that it became aglow from friction before he pressed it into the back of my neck (which would explain the chafing noise I heard directly before my unexpected blare of pain). That's when Mrs. Foxwood stopped her reading and asked me what happened. She seemed a trifle vexed at having her lesson interrupted and a little concerned. I told her that I thought I'd been stung by a bee, and that I was sorry (I knew the buzzing thing with the stinger was really a jerk named Jordan Saunders, but I kept my mouth shut). She asked if I wanted to go to the nurse, but I told her no, I would tough it out.

Did I mention the other kids in class as this was going on? No, I guess I didn't. First off, having the lesson interrupted is always something great for them since they are a bunch of cretins who don't appreciate good literature. And second, seeing a fellow classmate, me especially, in pain made them laugh as well. Call it human nature I guess, call it cynicism, call it whatever you want, but the underlying fact remains the same: Human nature is evil. They even laughed at me when I said I'd tough it out. I guess that could have been expected though.

That was my only confrontation with The Clan today.

Since it was an "A" day I didn't have Gym, which thankfully deprived Steve the opportunity to aim volleyballs at my head again. Steve *did* mock me, however, about my reddened neck in Health, asking me if I had been "stung" by a bee, but he didn't do anything after that. Mr. Cane had brought in a video that showed women and men naked, and I think that fixated his attention instead. I can't lie; my attention was diverted toward the screen as well. Believe it or not . . . and I'm almost sad to write this . . . it was the first time I saw the female body nude.

I guess I'm a late bloomer and never had any real interest in porn, but wow, that's all I have to say. The fabric of my sweat pants began to tighten, and I made sure that I stayed in my seat well after the video had been turned off.

Update on my parents:

They seemed the same at dinner, and I guess I should probably include a small blurb about them in each entry now, even though half the things I say I'm going to do fan out and eventually falter out of existence anyway. But for now, I'll include it.

My dad didn't ask about Dr. Murgelsy tonight. Instead he asked me about school, and how it was going. I told him fine. Then, my mom interrupted and asked about Gym class. I told her we're playing volleyball now and have baseball next quarter. I hate volleyball. Every time I think of that sport I see a big, white, panel-stitched ball go whizzing by my head and the leer of Steve Jones.

:::Shudders:::

~Peter

September 27, 20--
Wednesday

There was a fire drill during Social Studies today, and let me tell you that was probably the worst time it could have been since Social Studies is the one class where I encounter the whole Clan in one bout. To make matters entirely worse, John was absent. I later found out that he's got strep throat and won't be coming in for the rest of the week. This sucks. What will I do for the next two days without John in Social Studies and Health? I guess I'll soon find out.

When my school has a fire drill, the teachers line the students up in two single-file lines and escort them out the nearest exit. The goal of which is to garner and practice cooperation in case such an emergency ever presents itself. Which I might add will probably never happen. In my school's thirty years of existence—commemorated by the concrete plaque out front—no emergencies worth mentioning have ever happened. I once heard there was an uninvited gentleman wandering our halls, and the faculty had to announce "Mr. Rogers is in the building," but that's the worst that I know of and that was, from what I heard, back when the school first opened. Needless to say, we still practice these scenarios and that's where I found myself today: outside on the school's front lawn—near the flagpole where the 9/11 memorial service had been held—standing in a swarm of jabbering students. And amongst these students flew four bees, three of whom paid me a visit: Steve Jones, Jordan Saunders, and Casey Vector.

It was Casey who spotted me first, I think, because he was the one who initially came up to me. It was from behind as always. I felt something pointy being jabbed into my spine, and when I turned around, I saw that it was Casey's finger. *"What's up, Dough-boy? How them jelly rolls doing?"* he asked me. I didn't reply. I find that staying silent works better. At least if you're quiet, you can't give them anything new to mock you on. To the left and right of him stood Steve and Jordan, both of them with their arms crossed in front of their chests like some *Charlie's Angels* depiction. I even think one of them was leaning slightly back.

About ignoring someone: It's tedious work when you keep getting poked at or blown on, but in the end it's worth it. They ALWAYS get bored and walk away. Same as in this case. But before they did, Steve said, *"I'm going to get you, Pony-boy, don't forget that. You better watch your jelly rolls from now on."* I think that if I hadn't gone to the bathroom in Chem.—which was a nerve-racking task after what had happened there—I would have definitely wet myself, because in order to say this, Steve leaned in so close that I could feel the hot moisture of his putrid breath in my ear, and if he had wanted to he could have licked me with his tongue. That's how close he was.

:::Shudders:::

There was one other occurrence—one that could have been important. In Home Ec., I heard Sarah Kimble ask Katie what her mother and father did for a living. My ears shot up at once. I had to know. She was over by her counter with her group, and I guess Sarah had walked over to them and started the chitchat. Not that any of that mattered. What mattered was the information. At the time I didn't even know what I would do with it, if it would help me or not, but I knew I had to have it—if I found out I knew I could sleep easier.

Katie told Sarah that her father was an architect. In response, Sarah said something I can't remember. Then, as I strained my ears to listen to her articulate her mother's profession—Katie on the verge of saying it, me watching her lips spread apart to show her perfect white teeth—an uproar of laughter muffled her voice. It was like being deaf and watching television. Her lips moved, but without the captions it was useless.

Beside me, George Paterson had egg splatter all over his right hand and jeans. When I asked what had happened, Teddy Simone told me that Jessica Serino had told George that it was impossible to break an egg in your hand by squeezing it, that it was somehow geometrically impossible because of its shape (she of course referring to a perfect sphere, which of course an egg is not). It obviously wasn't impossible for George because he was braying excited laughter and shouting with triumph as the egg goo exuded between his clenched fingers. Mrs. Turner even came over to see what had happened, and when she did, Teddy told her that George had underestimated his strength. Jessica sighed.

I guess it was funny. I mean, I did chuckle a little, too, but I wish it didn't happen. I could have given up my laughter—the very few times it happens in school—to know the answer to the question that has been plaguing my mind since I became introduced to Dr. Murgelsy.

Them's the breaks as they say. Or in George Paterson's case . . . *Egg's* the breaks.

On to my parents:

Dinner was a bit different tonight. My dad didn't join us; it was just my mom and me. I got his call at about seven before I went upstairs to play WOW, and he said that he was staying late at the office to take care of some work for one of his accounts. He told me not to worry and that he'd be home much later tonight, probably after I had gone to bed, which, as it seems, is correct because here it is twelve a.m., and I still haven't heard the garage door open. He told me to tell my mom that she shouldn't make him dinner—I don't know if he intended that to be a sarcastic comment on her part or not but I relayed the message to hear her grunt. I think she knows something that I don't. Just the idea of my dad staying late to "work on his account" is very unsettling because I couldn't conceive him cheating on my mom. But when there is a divorce on the horizon anything is possible I guess. I just hope my life doesn't fall into the tread that theirs embedded before me.

By the way, my mom and I had pizza for a change, which was really awesome, and got my mind completely off the speculation of what my dad could be doing. The place the pizza came from was La Rosa, this Italian restaurant over on Trevnor Avenue. We had it delivered to the house nice and warm. Half the pie was barbecue chicken with steak sauce, the other was vegetable, with plenty of dressing. I have to say that the barbecue side was out of this world. It was a symphony of flavor. It was just that good!

Too bad my dad had to miss out, I'm sure he would have loved it. I think pizza is his favorite next to shepherd's pie. But with him at "work" doing "business things," it afforded my mom and me a chance to rekindle our own lost connection, even though I think it may have been as ersatz as the Van Gogh on our living room wall.

She talked to me about school and about the students, about Tommy Boots and John, and finally about Dr. Murgelsy. Once again, as I've become accustomed to doing, I fed her all the right answers. The expected answers. And she smiled.

How could I ruin a perfectly good dinner by bringing up Steve Jones? Plus, by the end of our conversation, I think she even took on somewhat of a genuine interest. Since she realized she didn't have to compete for my love with my dad, she eased up on all the extraneous questions and focused more on the ones that, I think, she really wanted to know the answers to. I answered them as truthfully as I could and it put me to pains to lie when I had to—it's a very rare occasion nowadays when I would ever get such an opportunity to "open up" to my mom.

I still haven't heard the garage door open yet . . .

~Peter

September 28, 20--
Thursday

John was absent again as I said he would be, and Social Studies was a throbbing headache with The Clan, but I seemed to manage. I pretty much ignored them until Mr. Clemmings walked into the room and started his lesson. Thank God Tommy Boots wasn't absent. I don't know what I'd do during lunch. Steve and his new disciples would surely have done something to me, maybe drag me into the bathroom and push the replay button on what he and the rest of The Clan did to John.

As far as an update on my parents: I didn't hear my dad come home last night. He was at dinner tonight and thanked me again for telling my mom that he had to "work late." He asked me a collection of questions to catch up on the past night and today. I gave him the same answers I gave my mom and watched as she just shook her head at various times in our conversation.

Maybe it was his ploy to do this. To skip a night of conversation and eat it all up the subsequent day, paralyzing my mom into silence as he swallowed up all forms of discussion. If that was the case, then he failed, because the split-second my mom saw an opportunity she jumped right in with her own question or comment, steering the conversation her way.

Needless to say, dinner tonight was a power battle. I finished early.

I'm in my room now. The steak sauce and ketchup taste still on my tongue, bits of beef from the burgers still stuck in the recesses of my teeth. Since my parents were doing a poor job at clandestinely fighting, I thought this the only sanctuary I could flee to. At least if I'm in my room they have to knock before entering.

Now that I have the time to think about it, I wonder if my dad even came home last night. I know he said he would after I'd gone to sleep but couldn't that have just been a lie to ease any suspicion that he was spending the night elsewhere? Could it even be possible that he's planning another life for after the divorce? My stomach does rolls at that notion. I don't want a stepmother; I love my own mom. I love my own dad. And I wish they would fix things.

I don't want to write anymore. I'll update you tomorrow on everything. And since I see Dr. Murgelsy I'm sure I'll have something interesting to say.

~Peter

September 29, 20--
Friday

What I had always feared happened: Tommy Boots was absent at lunch, and Steve Jones descended upon me. I knew I had something coming but I didn't really expect how bad it would be until it actually happened.

I didn't see him for more than half the period, and I thought I was getting away lucky when I caught sight of him and Gary Reith turning the corner, traversing from the east wing to the west wing. Beside them were Steve's two new disciples: Chris and Tim, replacing Jordan and Casey for the time being. I guess Gary couldn't miss out on this opportunity and got out of class on a bathroom pass.

As I caught sight of them, Chris Christianson and Tim Ridger flanked and pulled me up while Steve continued walking to the courtyard outside. Once again an inauspicious moment for me—the lunch aide wasn't at her post. And I guess if she were, Gary would have distracted her.

Dragging me past the reams of chattering students who were playing catch and handball, Steve's two disciples led me to the alcove around the building where the emergency door to the staircase dwelled. I knew screaming out would only make them angrier and apt to thrash me more so I stayed quiet. I didn't want to give them any satisfaction whatsoever, although I think they got plenty in the end anyway.

Steve said, and I remember this clearly, *"Here it comes, Jelly-rolls, you ready? I'm gonna bleed you of your cream filling!!!"*

His voice still echoes in my head.

I think that's when either Chris or Tim stomped on my foot, crushing my pinky toe. Or maybe it was after the first punch; I'm not sure and don't really want to try to remember. What I am positive about is the savage intensity all four of them used to throw their blows. Since I have a lot of padding, I guess they wanted to be sure that their punches got through. I can assure you that being fat does *not*, and I repeat, does NOT, help cushion a blow one bit; skin still bruises, pain receptors still transfer the information, and abrasions still bleed.

Like John, they avoided my face, but concentrated more so on my arms and legs—the parts I have less fat on. It was utterly horrible, and I think I moaned a great deal against my will. I just couldn't help it.

When they were done, Gary spat on my face and kicked me in the stomach, chasing the breath out of my lungs. It took me a full five minutes just to get it back as I lay looking up at the heavens wondering what God's plan was.

When I got home, Corolla was ready to take me to see Dr. Murgelsy. She noticed my limp and asked me what had happened. I told her I was playing baseball at lunch (an exaggeration of the boys playing catch which gave me the idea) and hurt my leg sliding into first, which is why I was so dirty as well. Little did she know it was because I had been dragged.

Corolla accepted it and smiled at the mention of me playing with boys other than Tommy Boots and John.

"Good job, Peewee, you see, it good to have friends," she said.

Right. If people like Steve Jones and Gary Reith were my friends, then who would need enemies?

Dr. Murgelsy questioned my limp as had Corolla. I think she was a little more disbelieving, but I convinced her in the end. At least I hope I did. She said that it was good to make other friends than your main ones. The richness of a person is not measured in gold but of his numeration of friends.

If that was the case then I'm probably the poorest kid in Farmsville High School.

She didn't dwell on that subject for too long—we played the *Witch Hunter* card game I brought along with me and later I showed and explained to her the fundamentals of WOW. I guess since my last visit, she purchased a membership and wanted to get involved. I'm glad that I can at least make a positive influence on somebody.

We didn't talk about my parents today either, but she did ask me if I was happy. At the time it sounded like such a stupid question—I lied, of course, and said life couldn't be better—but now that it's had time to simmer in my head I'm beginning to think about it.

Am I happy?

It's really a two-sided question. On one hand, I guess I am happy for the friends I have, for having parents who love me (even though they seem to be using me more as an object than a person), and for all the books and video games that have been created. But on the other hand, a lot of things could be better. For one, my parents could stay together, or more so, the whole concept of the divorce could have never presented itself in the first place; Steve Jones's parents never could have conceived him and the rest of The Clan could have followed suit of someone else; Katie Murgelsy and I could be dating; and I could be very athletic and attractive.

In a utopian society these things would exist, but that's not what the world is. The world is a dystopia, filled with equal measures of both good and evil: Add one tablespoon of religion, a pinch of government, mix and serve chilled.

I guess the only thing I can do is wait for my future to unfold and see where it will lead me. I'm sure I'll do something positive with my life. After all, writing this journal has made me consider the possibility of becoming a writer. Who knows, maybe I'll try my hand at fiction and see where that leads me.

On to my parents:

My limp. It was my mom who spotted it first as I approached the dinner table. I had a thought to go straight to Tommy Boots's house right after Dr. Murgelsy's but Corolla had insisted that we go to Stop and Shop and pick up a few things so my mom could make dinner. In all honesty, I never realized how long shopping could take. But on the plus side, I did get to pick out a few things that my mom normally overlooks: Drako's, Twinkies, Devil Dogs, etc. Maybe next time Corolla goes shopping, I'll go along with her again.

Back to dinner. When I was fully seated—wincing to myself and hiding it as best as I could—my mom inquired about my limp. I spun the tale as I had the first two times, and she said that she was proud of me as well, that it was good to get "physical exercise" during the school day, and how I should do it more often.

Right. I think I had all the physical exercise I could handle for the year.

It was a good thing that I'm wearing a long sleeved shirt because before sitting down to eat I took a shower and noticed just to what extent I had been bruised. Both my arms and legs and portions of my mid-reign are swathed in discoloration. If my mom had noticed that then she would have never believed my story about sliding into base.

After satisfying her questions about my limp, my dad asked me about class and what I was doing in Home Ec. I think he found it comical that I was taking that class, but he never fully came out and said it. When he brought this up, my mind immediately recalled the picture of George Paterson with the egg splatter all over him. God, how I want to know if Katie is related to Dr. Murgelsy! I don't think I'll ever get a more perfect opportunity to find out again, unless I ask her myself, and I certainly doubt that'll ever happen. Not even if we get paired up again.

My parents began bickering to one another more openly tonight. One complaint sprouted into two, and now it's only a matter of time before the whole plant buds. I really don't want to watch it grow and would deprive it of nourishment as best I could if I knew how, but I don't. With that being said, I excused myself from the table and here I am writing.

I think now that my entry is complete, I'm going to go over to Tommy Boots's. He and John are more than likely expecting me.

~Peter

September 30, 20--
Saturday

I didn't expect to sleep over Tommy Boots's last night, but one thing led to another and by the time we finished playing WOW, it was already two in the morning. I couldn't call my parents since they get up early as it is and decided to sleep there without their approval. I thought I would consider it a test to see if they're concerned parents or not. With that being said, I'll state that they failed with flying colors. Since I close my bedroom door when I'm in there, and since I close it when I leave as well, I don't think they even knew the difference. They probably just thought I came home late after they went to bed and was still sleeping when they woke up. This goes to show you how often they peek in to check on me. Don't normal parents do that every so often? I know if I had a son or a daughter my age, I would. I guess mine don't. Whatever. They have too much on their plate with the impending divorce and their constant verbal swordplay to take the time out and notice me. I understand. At this time in their life, I'm none other than a pawn used to either block, move, or exchange for something greater.

Since I decided to sleep over Tommy Boots's house, we fired his computer right back up and played WOW until five in the morning, continuing where we left off leveling his Toon.

When I woke in the sleeping bag he provided, it was two in the afternoon. The both of us got up and had breakfast before meeting with John on our bikes. I guess I didn't mention that John didn't sleep over. He called his mom, but she had sounded all groggy on the phone and nagged him to come home.

After we met up, we rode to Revina's Clutch, that sand pit I talked about earlier. We haven't been out there since June and whoever has been riding there recently built it up pretty nice. I did horrible and just wound up coasting around the embankments and over the humps. Every time a jump came up, I wound up going around it. John, however, got some extreme height on this one particular jump—the third in the set. I wish I had had my digital camera so I could have taken a picture of him mid-air and edited it in Photoshop. I could have added a nice caption and blown it up into a poster on my DesignJet.

After riding, I went to John's house for dinner. John's family was having ravioli and breadsticks, and it was awesome. I think it's really cool to be Italian, and I wish that I could have had that ethnicity instead of my Norwegian half. I might not even be so pasty if that was the case.

I had to stop home to check in with my parents after eating, and take a good shower. By then, it was eight, and they were eating in separate rooms. That's pretty much when I found out that they were completely oblivious to my not coming home last night. My mom stopped me on the way through the kitchen and told me flat out that I had come home too late, and that she wanted me to try to get home earlier on the weekends from now on, unless of course I was sleeping over. When her words reached my ears, I wasn't aware of my visage; I might have had an awestruck face or that of sudden grief. I don't even think I could tell you now how I feel about it. I'm stricken indifferent. I think it hurts, but I'm not sure. All that I was aware of was the invisible ball that welled in my throat, lodging itself so firmly against my airway that speech was a difficult task. The ball is still there as I write this now. It hurts to swallow. John is expecting me at his house tonight, but I don't think I'm going to arrive any time soon. I need to lie down and think. About what? I'm not entirely sure.

~Peter

October 1, 20--
Sunday

It steadily grows worse.

I think God hates me for not going to church. It's obvious now that my parents aren't going to go anymore and take me. I still pray extra upon waking every Sunday but I guess that's not enough.

Today, John, Tommy Boots, and I went out to the Bayview Mall. John's mom dropped us off as is the standard practice, and we spent most of the day there. Let me just say that I wish it was different, that possibly we could have been born a few years earlier—Tommy Boots a year—so that we could all have had our driver's licenses by now and left. Because halfway through our visit, I saw Steve Jones.

I can't even explain how awestruck I was. It was like having someone invade the sanctity of your home while you undressed for a bath.

And if that wasn't enough, Steve was not alone . . .

At first, I only saw the back of her head and assumed that somehow Steve had made the trip out there to meet up with some out-of-town girl. But when she turned around, I swallowed my heart. It was Katie Murgelsy. And they were at my mall. They were at MY mall! TOGETHER!

The feeling I felt is closely related to being stepped on

with a sharp pair of cleats. Like having that invisible ball lodged in your throat completely rob you of every struggling breath and choke you to death. Like being eaten, regurgitated, and pecked at by infected buzzards.

All hope as I knew it for Katie ended at that abrupt span of three seconds, when I saw her face next to Steve Jones's. My world came crashing down, and all I could think of was one solitary solemn question: Why? *Why?* WHY?

Tommy Boots saw the direction my face was pasted in, and, after calling my name twice and getting no response at all, he fixed his gaze parallel to mine and saw who I was looking at. I think his heart skipped a beat when he saw Steve, but he couldn't have had any idea of how I felt, how I still feel, because I didn't tell him or John about Katie. To them, she is just another face falling prey to another jock in Farmsville High School.

God, please give me the strength to get through this abomination.

Please give me the strength to find the will to move on.

And please give Katie the strength to wise up and reject the propaganda of the cretin known as Steve Jones.

Please.

~Peter

P.S. To make matters worse, my mom bought me a new baseball mitt. She said that since I was making new friends at school, a new mitt would help me improve my skills.

I couldn't even tell you how that made me feel.

October 2, 20--
Monday

Things just keep getting better.

It's her daughter. I'm positive now.

Corolla took me to Dr. Murgelsy's as scheduled, and she and I played WOW, the *Witch Hunter* card game I was asked to bring, and afterwards we did something we usually don't do: We talked. I'm not sure how or why it happened, I think maybe either I said something or she did something that made one of us inquire about something else, but it led to us talking. And from her ramblings I was able to determine that the daughter of which she spoke of was none other than Katie.

The similarities were too coincidental for it not to be—the age, the moving into a new school district, and the new guy she was dating. Ugggh. DATING!

I wanted to throw up.

I couldn't believe it, yet I could at the same time. Didn't I have the feeling ever since I first met with Dr. Murgelsy that she was Katie's mother? Didn't I view them as similar individuals? I most certainly did, and yet it still comes to me as a complete surprise.

I knew that my chances of dating Katie were nil from the start, but now the chances of us even becoming just friends are completely shot as long as Steve is whispering propaganda in her ears.

Through one of the many of the books I've read, the same message is conveyed: Love is blind. What this amounts to is that the person shot by Cupid's arrow has a cloud covering their eyes of the true demeanor of the person they view as their loved one. Their veiled vision does not allow them to discern the true form of how this person exists. It is shrouded by a feeling they *think* they feel for them. Only when it is too late—after the breaking up and the bloodletting of love—does the arrow-punctured person view their now ex-lover in their true wolf-in-sheep's-clothing form and realize that they have wasted whatever time they have invested into the relationship.

This is going to happen to Katie.

She is going to fall head first for this maniacal jock, this ersatz Romeo.

Steve is going to be the one who hires the hit man, Cupid.

And Steve is going to be the one to recruit this once empathic girl into his Clan, the first and foremost of the female division aimed at making my life a living hell.

All is lost.

~Peter

October 3, 20--
Tuesday

Dinner was horrible tonight. In fact, my parents are still downstairs eating. I just couldn't stand to sit with them any longer. My mom was talking to me about school, when my dad interrupted, asking his own questions. She got angry and told him to "shut his trap" when she was talking to me. And since they don't hide their emotions anymore, he did the opposite: He screamed at her. I sunk down in my chair, hoping to turn invisible.

The only thing I could do was leave.

And here I am, in my room, while downstairs my parents continue their argument. I think the only way to escape their fighting is to lose myself in my writing.

Today, I saw Katie walking with Steve in the hall. They were holding hands. Again, seeing this stabbed my heart with Cupid's arrow, this one dipped in arsenic rather than the potion of love.

I saw her doodling on her notebook in French class as all girls who are in love do. Love is such a strong word in this case, so I'll only use the word *"crush."* As in I hope she crushes Steve's heart when she realizes he's playing her for a fool, that he does not have one romantic bone in his body.

I think if I ever saw them kiss, I would throw up.

And to think I wanted to marry Katie. How could this once-dreamed-of bride of mine want to go and get hitched up with a person like Steve? What could she possibly see in him? I know I can't compare in looks, but c'mon, the guy has no personality. He's a marionette being dangled by

WAIST Of A
LIFE!

PETER RABIT!
Jelly Gut.

October 11, 20--
Wednesday

I don't even know how to begin this entry. So many things have happened since I last wrote that I think I almost went crazy with your absence. An atomic warhead crashed and vomited its shrapnel of aspersions upon me when I saw you in Steve Jones's hands. My stomach twisted into a tight little ball and that metaphorical lump in my throat returned, transmogrifying into something real, nearly killing me.

Thank God I got you back, thank God! No, let me reconsider that. I *HATE* God. Better yet, there is no God. I got beat up again and was left lying face up, staring at the God-less heavens—that of which I am now *fully* convinced. Forget the story of Job and God's bet with Satan. These horrors DO NOT mean that God must love me. *"Blessed is* NOT *the one whom God corrects."* More so, I don't believe he exists at all. No, I RESENT god and the whole idea of him. There, notice anything different? ~~gggggg~~od. How can god exist if he would let such a macabre act befall upon one of his children? An act, no, a plague, that is veiled under the names of Steve Jones and The Clan? The answer is simple, and I now pain myself to think that I actually believed he had a plan for my life, something that would soon turn all this turmoil into good.

I was wrong. He does not exist, and if he does, the

bastard absolutely hates me.

If he existed, you, my journal, would not have fallen into Steve Jones's hands; god would have intervened and done something to prevent that. I should blame myself for this truthfully, but if god was as benevolent as they say he is then he *could have* done something that would have prevented it. Ugggh! Look at what they did to you, they SCROLLED MALICIOUS RED SLANDER ACROSS YOUR WHITE PAGES, DREW WICKED AND IMMORAL PICTURES THROUGHOUT MY DEEPEST AND DARKEST FEELINGS, and they read you . . . THEY READ YOU!

There are dirty finger prints on numerous pages, one corner that looks to have been pissed on—fouled by urine, the excretion of the most impure defilement. And they read you . . . THEY READ YOU!

I can't get that picture out of my head. Oh g— They read you!

My life as I know it in school is over. My deepest darkest fears and my long-shot aspired hopes have been dispersed throughout the student body, and I am now a laughing legend at Farmsville High School. Most would want to be remembered for the rest of their lives as one scribed down in the books for ages to come, but it's reverence that they strive to achieve not the antithesis—not what I have achieved.

My life is over.

And I have nobody to blame but myself. Nobody but

myself. Which is the worst horror of all. If I could place blame on another, it would possibly unclasp these restricting bands of metal around my lungs and remove my head from the guillotine, but I can't; it was my own fault and the act of unfortunate coincidences.

The last time I saw you in my house was when I was writing last Tuesday. If I flip back a few pages I can see exactly where I left off and could probably finish that entry, but what would be the point? Life changed, and so has my views about it. But it was during that day, that night of October the third, that set the stage for what was about to happen: During my writing of that entry, I heard footsteps coming up the stairs. As I've written before, my mom and dad knock before entering my room; this was not the case that night. I judged by the intense plodding of feet that whomever they belonged to was not going to stop at my door, instead they were going to open it and barge right in. It made sense why, my mom was crying and I ended up comforting her. She and Dad's fight had escalated after I left the dinner table, and she said that he had actually hit her. I don't know how much to believe; if she provoked him to do it, whether she's lying or is being truthful on the matter, but she was upset. I had to console her.

As the doorknob started to turn my heart skipped, and I started. I didn't know what to do with my journal so I did the only thing I could do and tossed it in my backpack, which was open on the bed. I, of course, had every intention to take it out as soon as my mom left—I would never even think about taking it to school—but she stayed longer than I expected, and by the time she left, I was over-tired and my eyes were closing. I had forgotten, and that's where my fault lay.

I had forgotten.

At some point the next day, I must have somehow dropped the very book I now write in out of my backpack . . . or maybe Jordan Saunders took it out in English class. I'm not sure. I honestly don't even know how I didn't see it sitting in my backpack when I threw my lunch bag in it. It just goes to show you that the mind can be oblivious to things unless it is in search of them.

Later, when I got home and did my daily business, I decided to write. It was then that I was stricken with my worst fear: I didn't know where I had put my blessed journal. I tore my room apart looking for it, then remembered my mom coming in the night before and how I threw it in my backpack. But I was more than sure I had taken it out. I even searched my bag when I realized it was missing. My mind was racing. I got hot flashes like a menopausal woman. I looked for it for hours on end. Hours. I was distraught when the search yielded nothing. I believe it's veracious to say that my hopes and dreams were crushed that very night.

I didn't find out until this Thursday—the fifth—that Steve Jones had it the whole time. As I was sitting at lunch with Tommy Boots, Steve stood up in the middle of the west wing cafeteria and thumbed open the page of a book which I immediately recognized and began to read. My heart stopped, and I was unsure if it would ever beat again—Steve was dictating my journal, dictating its inner secrets to all who would listen. I can't even write what I did next because I honestly don't remember. I might have fainted or blacked out or I might have sat there with big gaping voids as eyes. Next to me, Tommy Boots put two and two together and realized Steve Jones was reading my journal. He never asked why I didn't tell him about it, only saw my face that day and understood all.

He even tried to get it back. I remember that clearly and can't thank him enough for it—he was going after his greatest fear for a friend. He was grabbed by Tim Ridger and Chris Christianson and that pretty much ended his futile attempt. The lunch aide was AWOL from her post yet again, and Tommy Boots and I were dragged out to that familiar alcove by the emergency door that I had come to know and hate. There both he and I—he for the first time, me for the second—got to relive what I had gone through in that very same spot twelve days ago.

The next day, before Mr. Clemmings entered the room, most of The Clan was sitting, not in their seats across the room, but in mine. And in Steve Jones's hand was my journal. He was reading more entries and actually ripped half of one of them, crumpled it up into a ball, spit on it, and threw it at me. It struck me in the temple and I could do nothing but stare dumbfounded as they continued to read my secret thoughts.

In the hall that week, I saw Katie clinging onto Steve more and more, and one of the times my journal was splayed open between them. She was giggling.

Later that day, I could barely find the strength to go to Mrs. Rugerrielli's French class. When I did, I was late. Probably not the smartest thing because everyone always looks at the late person. As I walked to my desk—my eyes giving the floor a visual inspection—I saw in my peripheral that Katie was snickering at me. In Home Ec., she was downright laughing with Sarah Kimble, and I will give you three guesses as to what or whom they were laughing at.

This Monday Gary Reith had my journal in his possession during Health. I saw him doodling in it with a marker, and I could only shed a tear. John saw this and felt for me, or so I had thought, because when Gary handed it back to Steve, and he began to read the entry where I mentioned my parents call me Peter Rabbit, John actually laughed. I couldn't believe it. One of my best friends actually laughed at something I had written. John told me he didn't laugh at that, that it was something else his mind drew up, but I'm not stupid. I even saw him walking next to Steve yesterday and overheard Steve asking him: *"Why do you hang out with that loser anyway? You know, if you stopped hanging out with him, we wouldn't pick on you as much."* My heart sank, and I began to cry in the hall. I think, but am not sure, that Steve also said: *"You're not like him. You stood up to Jordan."*

All this happened in that

I'm sorry, I fouled your page with my tears. I don't deserve a book as good as you to harbor my feelings. My one escape from reality . . .

I'm worthless.

Let me regroup.

All this happened in the time span from the third up until today. Thankfully—I don't know how or why—I found you, my journal, lying under the lunch table when the cafeteria was clearing out. Maybe irony struck and Steve lost you the same way I had, maybe not. I'm not sure. All I know is that I now have my precious journal back in my possession and I can write this:

I honestly don't know what to do anymore. I think there is only one option left for me—one way out. And that is suicide. Since I don't believe in god anymore, I don't consider it a sin now. Would the world really miss me? I doubt it. I can't do it at home, it wouldn't leave a big enough impression, and I wouldn't want my parents to find my body. It will have to be at school. I will have to write a note and explain why, explain how, Steve Johns and The Clan drove me to this decision. That it's the only way to stop this pain that is festering on my soul.

Goodbye...

~Peter

October 12, 20--
Thursday

It's so hard.

The thought of suicide is both soothing and frightening. I'm not sure I could even bring myself to do it, or if I could, find a means to accomplish it in a way that could make a statement. Another one of life's paradoxes.

As I said: *It's so hard.*

In Chem., I spoke with John and told him I saw him walking with Steve Jones. At first, I think I caught him by surprise, but he covered it up when he told me flat out that he *was* walking with him. He said that he had a great idea—a plan. It was that if he started to get "in" with Steve and the rest of The Clan, then he could influence them not to pick on any of us anymore. I looked at him as if he had five heads, but Tommy Boots agreed with him by saying that might not be a bad idea. I argued with them both, questioning why The Clan would possibly let John into their little club or whatever they like to call themselves, and if in fact he could get in, why? What would The Clan have to gain? I told them both that I didn't mind getting picked on, that I'd suffer for the most part and allow The Clan to focus all their attention on me if they wanted to. It was an outright lie, but John didn't answer.

The period after, I was hit directly in my eye with a

spitball. If I could write only one thing about getting hit in the eye with a spitball, it would be that it HURTS! I'm not talking about the eyelid or the lashes, but right on the cornea. As soon as I felt the sharp presence of something invading my eye's sanctity I closed it and began rubbing it. It turned beet-red and stung for the rest of the day—still stings now.

I'm beginning to dislike Mr. Clemmings. He's never in his room before class and is always late. Other kids in the class like to throw quarters across the room, hitting the radiator, and making a huge ruckus. I never once participated. Not once! And here I was feeling sorry for the man whose pre-class absences always contributes to my hazing, to getting beaten up and spit at with spit balls? Psssh! I HATE him!

Then, as if that wasn't enough, Steve Jones, Jordan Saunders, and Casey Vector, portraying a trio, shouted, *"PETER RABBIT!"* at the top of their lungs and brayed unstoppable laughter.

Again my heart dropped. They had gotten that out of my journal along with plenty of other things.

The only good thing was that the class wasn't full yet and I wasn't *completely* humiliated. I shot John a glace and he looked away. I don't think his plan is to benefit me at all, but rather to benefit himself. He always held that selfish quality, and I think he might have found a small aperture in the high school caste system and is going to slither his way through its slimy walls by any means necessary, even if that means playing Brutus and stabbing me in the back. Who knows if this is even possible. Let's say it is and if by some one-in-a-million chance he *does* get "in" with The Clan, how does he think they are going to treat him? Certainly not like their own. More like that second-rate piece of dog turd, a lapdog to entertain themselves with. But I guess, in his eyes, if it will get him a date for junior and senior prom in the years to follow, then it's all worth it.

I hope I'm just losing lucidity and none of that will happen. I keep picturing John laughing as Steve read those words—*Look how our Peter Rabbit is growing up!*—and my heart keeps sinking. Aren't your friends supposed to stand by your side? To support you by any means necessary? Tommy Boots did and still is thankfully, but I don't know about John. If god existed I could pray to him, but he doesn't, and if he did he wouldn't hear my prayer anyway.

~Peter

October 13, 20--

Friday

Friday.

Friday the 13th.

The day says it all.

I've stopped caring. Actually, that can't entirely be true. If it were, then I would have stopped writing as well, and I haven't.

Today I had to go see Dr. Murgelsy, but before I talk about my time with her, I want to recap school. In Math, Gary Reith flew another one of The Clan's famous paper airplanes over to me. When I opened it, I saw a picture that was scrawled to look like a copy of the one in this very journal (they're never going to let me live it down). Under it, they wrote KILL YOURSELF!

How can somebody who lost their father in 9/11 be so inconsiderate of other peoples' feelings? If something immoral could fall out of the sky or crawl out of a deep, dark crevice in the earth, I could only hope it would tear the throat out of either Steve Jones or Gary Reith first, before continuing on its rampage, destroying all of humanity.

Katie was absent today. I found myself able to see the board directly for the first time in French. I like it better this way. No seductress to cloud my thoughts throughout the period and my day. We had a surprise quiz, and despite the absence of the temptress, I believe I failed it. I haven't been studying since I lost my journal, and everything academically related in school has been a complete nebulous. The only good thing—if you could even call it good (maybe just indifferent now)—was that I didn't get beat up today.

At Dr. Murgelsy's, she asked me if I was feeling okay. She said that I looked distant. Yeah, only if she knew how distant I really was, that I was contemplating suicide at the very moment she conversed with me. I wonder how she would have taken that if I told her. I bet she would have been utterly surprised. Maybe I should have, maybe she could have helped. I doubt it though. She's just another grown-up that doesn't understand.

I'm torn between the decision of whether I should go over Tommy Boots's house tonight or not. I had originally told him that I wasn't feeling well, but when he said that John was out with his grandma and that he would be bored alone, it almost made me change my mind. The main reason behind me not wanting to go at first was of course the fact that John would be there. I still don't feel like seeing him right now, just as I didn't feel like seeing my parents argue at dinner. I was about to say yes when the thought struck me . . . his grandma? It's a Friday night at ten thirty p.m. The old lady would undoubtedly be sleeping. Instantly, Steve Jones's face popped into my head, and I told Tommy Boots that I couldn't go over his house, that I had to hang up and throw up. I actually did.

John hanging out with Steve Jones outside of school? Was it possible? I don't know.

I hope not.

Despite my sickness, my stomach is still gargling for food. I can't go down to the kitchen, though, I just might see one of my parents on the couch again and that might drive me to accomplish what I've been contemplating. That, and the mental image of Steve Jones.

~Peter

October 14, 20--
Saturday

Today was a thought day. I didn't go out and didn't pick up the phone when I saw Tommy Boots's father's name on the caller ID. I think I've drawn inside myself. And what could I expect? If you were going to kill yourself, wouldn't you draw away from the outside world, too? One less thing to miss and remember.

My thoughts are rocking back and forth and are becoming more disturbed than a long-tailed cat in a room full of rockers. I never thought like this before in all my life and it scares me. It really scares me.

Life.

Death.

Life.

Death.

The words are the direct opposites of one another. One is so final while the other is so continual. The options are none other than fifty-fifty. The only choice is: Which one do I choose?

I'm swimming in a pool of thought right now.

I'm confused.

I can't swim.

And there are no life preservers or floatation devices.

I'm drowning . . .

~Peter

October 15, 20--
Sunday

I believe I've made a decision.

It didn't come all at once, and it is still not definite, but reading my journal from first page to present and looking at the condition that has become of it and of the pains that I have endured, one thing is clear: I didn't put myself into this situation, someone else threw me into it.

Even though I am fully aware of the fact that every man is *not* born equal, every man is still born with a clear mind. My mind has been flooded with countless episodes of maltreatment ever since the fifth grade, and it seems to me that it's something of amazement that I have endured it for so long without it changing my persona. Maybe I have drawn into myself and avoided talking to my fellow classmates because of it, but I have never had an outbound rage to hurt them or myself, that is, until now. It's very confusing and I don't make sense to myself anymore. All I know is that one thing is standing out in flashing red lights:

It is what I must do.

I had originally left the drawings on the blank pages because I didn't think I could stand to rip a page out of the one thing that has helped me cope with my inner feelings. Now, I leave them as a reminder of what I must do, as courage to go forth and not back down. I have to get back at them. I'm not sure how, but I am positive that that is what has to be done. My reputation and life may be ruined and crumbling at the escarpment—me falling, tumbling, awaiting the inevitable crash at the bottom.

Death.

But I *can* help others. I can set an example for others in my position.

I don't know where this sudden burst of dauntlessness came from. Maybe it's because I have lost everything. EVERYTHING. And it's only after we've lost everything that we're free to do anything. All I know is that I must utilize it while it is there. I must grab the fire with my hands and hold onto it—despite the layers of my flesh crisping, charring, and melting—before I lose it and can never grasp it again.

I have to do something.

But what?

~Peter

October 16, 20--
Monday

Steve tripped me today, and I got up and walked away. I know something is coming, something big, but I'm not sure what it is yet. The only change is that it's going to be coming from my side this time and not his. I can feel it curdling my blood. Rage is the word I'm looking for. It surges through my veins each time I think of him, each time I see Katie and him together.

Today, I saw them kissing in the hall, and I just wished that someone could have accidentally tripped into them and made them bite each others' tongues off.

How could a girl that worked with me on a project—the one girl that actually spoke to me in my high school career—turn out to be so mean due to the influence of one person? Today, she snickered again as I sat behind her. And I think I heard her whisper "Pee-wee" as I sat down. She hasn't yet, but I'm almost certain that either she or Steve will bring up her mother to me; it's only a matter of time before that little piece of information gets spilled—Peter Rubin, the kid who sees a psychologist.

I'm finding that my usual way of coping doesn't ease my pain anymore. I'm finding myself drawing all the depression into a rage, along with malevolent thoughts.

It works. It feels better.

Tonight, before this entry, I wrote my very first work of fiction. It's short even compared to that of Edgar Allen Poe, but it quelled my anger. I'll transcribe it now:

STEVE JONES GETS WHAT HE DESERVES

BY PETER RUBIN

Steve Jones, a bully at Farmsville High School, sat in the pale blue chair in the west wing of the school's cafeteria. He sat flanked by his two disciples, Chris and Tim. They were new to him, like the repetitive incoming teeth are to sharks, and he knew how to treat them. His goal for the day was to pick on one student and one student alone: Peter Rubin.

Peter is a quiet boy who is often overlooked in the high school. Once or twice the bullies pick on him, but most often he keeps to himself and transcribes his thoughts in his journal.

One day, when Peter was eating and writing in his journal—pencil in one hand, plastic fork in the other—Steve Jones came up to him and tried a hand at his bullying. Peter contested Steve's rouse by asking him to leave him alone and by stating that he did not want to go outside to "look at the sky." He knew very well what was in the sky—a godless horizon and a quilt of rain-filled clouds. Soon the clouds would open and wet him just as Steve Jones had hoped Peter would wet his pants.

"C'mon, Jelly-rolls," Steve shouted to Peter. "Get your jelly-

gut outside and look at the sky."

"No," said Peter. "I won't." *And in that instant Peter thought of the Three Little Pigs and their verbal argument with the Big Bad Wolf. I won't. Not by the hair on my chinny chin chin.*

In Peter's mind, he was the little pig, and Steve Jones was the Big Bad Wolf. He had come to blow his house in. Peter couldn't let the wolf do that, for his house was his journal, and his journal was his house.

Steve whined and whined and shouted aspersions at Peter until his voice was hoarse, yet Peter did not budge from his seat. His hands had taken a white knuckling grip on the pencil and the plastic fork and his teeth had begun to grind, but he still would not move.

It was then that Steve decided he would try his luck at reaching for Peter's journal.

A muscular hand reached forth and groped the journal's spine. To Steve the touch must have felt like magic, like unclasping a girl's bra for the first time. It must have been that way because it was something that was so forbidden just as the illustrious apple had been to Eve in a tale that did not happen.

No sooner than Steve's fingers made contact, they soon drew back in a trail of blood, for Peter had gouged a deep hole into Steve's forearm with his pencil. Steve wailed in great pain and groped at the pencil. It was then that Peter stood up and with his free hand clasped the back of Steve's head and plunged the plastic fork into his eye. Viscid goo exuded forth, spilling onto his cheek and the bridge of his nose. His cries became an ululation of both pain and surprise. He floundered about the cafeteria, momentarily blinded by pain in his remaining eye. He stumbled over a chair and fell to the floor. The pencil in his forearm delved itself deeper and broke, graphite swimming its way up his bloodstream and into his heart.

The last words that Steve muttered before he died were: "I'm sorry."

I know it sounds very dark, but it made me feel better. If only something like that could actually happen to him. Not so horrible . . . no! As horrible. He deserves it. He has single-handedly ruined my life from the beginning of fifth grade.

I wish I could have moved; it would have saved me a lot of trouble.

As this change happened in my means of coping, coincidently so did the routine at Dr. Murgelsy's office. Today, she asked me about school instead of playing games. This was the first time she's done this since I've been seeing her. Originally I had thought she was tiptoeing her way around the mental barrier I had set up, but as the sessions progressed, and she didn't question me on my parents, I simply guessed she was lazy and found it easier to play games instead. Now I know that isn't the answer. She *was* tiptoeing since the beginning, first gaining my trust, then readying to strike. Waiting like a snake in the grass.

I wasn't ready to tell her anything.
When she asked about school, I lied.

~Peter

October 17, 20--
Tuesday

Before dinner, I discovered something I wish I hadn't. I'm not sure why I was looking, perhaps it was my inquisitive nature or my newfound way of coping with things, I'm not sure, but I looked and I found evidence. I've read that *if you don't want to know, you shouldn't look* (peek not through a keyhole, lest ye be vexed), and now I find the truth in that apothegm.

What I looked at was my dad's cell phone. It was on the counter in-between the den and the kitchen like it always is at night. When my dad went upstairs to change before dinner, I took it. Looking at it, I found numerous calls received and made to a woman named Miranda. Who the hell is Miranda?

My dad's cheating on my mom. It's the only sensible answer to all the calls on his phone. I doubt he'd call a business associate that much, and the chances of them being a female are too coincidental. I'm just thankful I didn't check the pictures on it. I don't think I could have dealt with seeing this woman's face if she was on there. In all probability it was, and it's my guess that this is whose house my dad was at the night he had to "work late."

Consequently, dinner was horrible after viewing and putting back my dad's phone. I didn't touch the cabbage stew my mom made, instead I kept thinking back to that one name, trying to draw a picture from it: *Miranda.*

I wonder what would have happened if it had been my mom who saw the name instead of me. Would she have actually plunged *her* fork into my dad's eye instead of me shoving it into Steve's in my story? I don't know. The only thing I know is that I'm torn between emotions.

This man is my dad. I love him, yet I hate him. I feel empty. There's not even a rage at this point anymore. I'm once again stoic.

I am an empty vessel.

~Peter

October 18, 20--
Wednesday

Steve "Jock-boy" Jones drove me to do it! He heaved a volleyball directly at my head, and it smashed into the side of my face, turning it bright red from what Tommy Boots said. Everyone in class laughed, and I felt anger surge through my veins. And I did something that I never thought I'd do in my life—I did what John did to Jordan Saunders, only my attempt wasn't quite as effective. Steve saw me coming and planted a foot out, and I fell face first over it. My chin smashed into the floor and I bit my tongue. I can still taste the blood in my mouth a little. And if I move my tongue against my teeth, I can feel the part where the raw skin is.

Everyone laughed at me. They *all* pointed and laughed at me, and that only made my rage deepen. And I couldn't alleviate it. I couldn't do anything. The one thing I tried backfired and made everything worse. I'm a complete lummox. My life is lost. Or so I had thought.

That's when I was struck by *the idea* a period later. I was heckled by Steve and the rest of The Clan in Social Studies but that has nothing to do with *the idea.* It came to me when Mr. Clemmings asked us to open our notebooks. As I flipped to the half-written page that I had started writing yesterday's notes on, I flipped through the beginning pages of the year, more specifically the notes on WWII. And as I was flipping through those pages a single name stood out:

ADOLF HITLER

Hitler had caused so much trouble in World War II with his genocide and anti-Semitism, but he had still led the whole Nazi party at his command. He had drawn them up by the sheer implement of speech. If this man could speak out and arouse a whole nation to follow his orders then mayhap I could, too. How? I have no idea. I'm not talking about genocide or even a single killing—even though I wish Steve Jones would die—but my thoughts were at that moment that I could learn something from him.

Five hours later, I was enduring the grueling task of pedaling my bike to Borders where I bought *Mein Kampf*, or, in its English translation: *My Struggle.*

If only Hitler knew of *my* struggle.

Now I stare at his autobiography upon my bed. I feel almost morally wrong for buying something that a sick, malicious deviant wrote, but he probably had reasons behind his actions as I do. I will begin to read it at the close of this entry and will soon find out what they were, as well as enrich my mind on how one man could possibly control a whole country of soldiers, to turn them against a whole religion. I only need to turn my school against four people. On second thought, throw Chris Christianson and Tim Ridger in there, too. Six people, I need to turn my school against six people.

Teach me, Hitler.

~Peter

October 19, 20--
Thursday

School sucked, and I found out in French that I had been walking around the hall between periods with three pencils stuck in my curly hair. My guess now is that Jordan did it in English since he sits behind me. At first, I had thought that the kids were snickering because of what Steve had read aloud in my journal, but as I walked on I became more curious. Every single person I passed laughed. I doubted that every one of them could have heard about the journal—news travels fast in high school, but not that fast.

When I walked into French, Katie dropped her head between her arms and cawed out laughter. Ms. Rugerrielli pulled me aside and whispered in my ear about my new hairpiece. I felt my face turn beet-red like the boiling of anger in an animated cartoon; it rose from my neck all the way to my forehead and would have blown the hair off my head (pencils in it and all) if it were not firmly attached to my skull by the scalp.

I *hate* Jordan Saunders!

It just gives me more reason to finish reading *Mein Kampf.* Last night I got a hundred pages in and am not surprised to say that the man knows how to write. It's now obvious why Hitler's propaganda was swallowed by a whole nation—he has a way with words. There is one thing that he says that stands out in my mind. I found it so influential that I had to write it down: *"Obstacles do not exist to be surrendered to, but only to be broken."* I believe he was referring to the obstacles of losing his mother and father and trying to become a famous architect and painter. But I think it's open for interpretation.

I must now look at my obstacles—The Clan—and rise up above them. They don't exist for me to surrender to as I have done in the past, they exist for me to conquer: to break the hold they have on others who view them as "cool." If a painter could rise up to become the most influential speaker of Germany in the early 1900s, then surely I could rise up above a group of four or six kids that torment me. All I have to do is believe. I have a new resolve for my life.

I will ***not take*** anymore of their bullying!

~Peter

October 20, 20--
Friday

Dr. Murgelsy agreed with me that it is important to begin to take matters into your own hands, to deal with the troubles that face you. No, I didn't tell her how I must rise above The Clan and find some way to turn my school against them. She simply thought I was talking about my parents. I know I said I wouldn't disclose any information to her, but I figured that I could trust her in a half-sense: by hearing her advice, but with her thinking it's about something completely different. I know that probably defeats the purpose but I wanted more reassurance. And I got it.

She asked about my parents again and that's how our whole conversation started. She asked if I was happy. I told her I was indifferent. She said that was impossible. I asked her how would she know. She responded by stating that *her* parents had gotten a divorce when she was pregnant with her child (that spiteful Plastic, Katie). She said it had hit her hard, especially at that point in her life—back then older couples weren't getting divorces as much and it took her by complete surprise, kind of like me. She said that she understood what I was going through, and that if I wanted to talk about it with her, she would be there to listen to me. I gave her my thanks and told her that I probably would take her up on that offer but not right now. In all honesty, I'm not sure what to do. I had no idea that she was a product of divorce like I will soon be myself. I guess that if I *could* talk to anyone about it the most logical person would be her. And she's not so bad. After all we do play WOW and *Witch Hunter* together. How many adults can I say that about? I don't know if I want to, though.

It's a hard choice to decide.

I think I'll muse over it while I sit home tonight.

I talked to Tommy Boots, and he said that it was John's house for the sleepover. I haven't said anything to John about the matter of The Clan since Tommy Boots mentioned he was out with his grandma. I don't know Steve Jones's intentions, but I do know of his venomous mind and propaganda. It turned Katie into a Plastic, and it will soon turn John against me, too, maybe already has. I can only give my thanks that he hasn't gotten to Tommy Boots. I'm sure in time John will try to bring him over to the dark side but by then I hope to have my plan in action. Tommy Boots is smarter than that, and I can only hope he'll make the right decision. I think he sees through my ruse of not going out. I told him I wasn't feeling well and that I had to catch up on some reading for an assignment. I know I shouldn't *hope* and should rather *do*, but I'm not sure as to what my plan of action will be just yet. The thought of suicide hasn't left my mind but I know for sure now that it is not the option I want to take. It's the easy way out—the surrendering method. And one that I cannot, no, *will not,* succumb to.

In time, when I know what I must do, I will tell Tommy Boots, and he'll talk to John. Right now, though, I can't see him. He'll only remind me of Steve, and if for some reason he mentions that cretin's name I might just explode in a fit of uncapped rage. Either that or cry. Most likely the former if I look at the way I've been coping lately.

I seem to be rambling now and what good does that do? I have a job to accomplish. I must finish as much as *Mein Kampf* tonight as I can. Only upon its completion will I be able to develop a better understanding of the man who led a revolution.

If I keep a steady pace, I think I might be able to finish all 688 pages by tomorrow night.

Wish me luck.

~Peter

October 21, 20--
Saturday

I was up until three reading yesterday and only have another 300 pages to go. I think I'll finish it after this entry. Let me first tell you about today.

After much debate, I found myself riding to the Sun Valley Mall. I know I've written that I'd never go to that mall because of obvious reasons, but as I've also stated, I've stopped caring. What more can I possibly lose? I've already lost my dignity, and I've never had any respect to begin with. I did, however, think of the possibility of getting jumped again, but I've endured plenty in my life already and what would one more instance be? Maybe it'd even add fuel to my fire to coerce me to establish my own type of movement against The Clan and all who support them in my school.

I rode the six miles to the mall and locked my bike on the bike rack. To my surprise I didn't bump into or see anyone from my school. I guess that just goes to show you the irony of it—in the past I've been going an hour out of the way by car to avoid the people I hate and wound up bumping into the worst of them anyway, where instead, I could have gone ten, and avoided them in the first place.

When I stepped through the entrance I noticed that the mall was flooded with Halloween decorations. Orange

Halloween lights, streamers hanging from the ceiling, pumpkins, and jack-o'-lanterns. It was very festive. They even had this one store called Halloween Scene. I went into it and looked at all the masks. There was even one of Charles Manson. How I wish I could have hid my face behind a permanent mask my whole life. In a sense, perhaps I did; my true feelings were never revealed and I never rebelled.

After Halloween Scene, I went into Hot Topic, this Goth store. Taking a long look at myself in the mirror I came to realize that maybe one of the reasons I've been picked on so long is the fact that Corolla has bought my clothes since before I could remember. Each student in school falls into their own type of category, their clique, and most prominently shows it by their appearance. Goths—always dress in black. Punks—dyed hair. Skaters—baggy jeans. Jocks—collared Polo shirts. And last but not least myself—the clothes Corolla buys me: tight sweat pants and sweaters. Her thoughts behind the sweats were no doubt the fact that they'd stretch to accommodate my weight, which was true. I've had the same ten pairs for the past three years, and I'll add that they didn't start off tight—I pretty much grew into them as I got fatter. However, if I'm going to do something, stand up for myself and try to have a movement of my own against The Clan, then I have to be taken seriously and start dressing different. Maybe the fact that everyone in school is now aware of me isn't altogether a bad thing—being known as a pushover is better than being nameless in this circumstance, right? Maybe it'll allow my voice to be heard—even if at first they only laugh. Hitler surely didn't accrue all his followers after the first speech he gave.

The question then arises: *What do I dress like?* There are so many styles, but I think the reason I was drawn to Hot Topic is because of its dismal appearance. The store is always swathed with tapestries and lighted in somber red lights. It portrays how I feel inside. I can almost relate to its atmosphere—it's a projection of my inner self.

After trying on seven pairs of pants and elatedly realizing that most of them actually fit, I bought four pairs with the money I had left over from my allowance. They're not completely out-there with the chains and straps like some of their contenders, but they have a *Notice me!* sort of look. As far as shirts, I bought a few hoodies of bands I've never heard of—all black. I know they say vertical stripes are sliming but black is devoid of color and will express the deepest sorrow of myself better.

At first, I thought that going to the mall by myself would be an utter recession of cheerfulness—in reality, quite the contrary. I found myself able to breathe more freely and allow my thoughts to progress at their own pace. No need to rush or quickly contemplate them so that I may return a comment—just natural speed. I found my mind musing over The Clan and what I must do about them. Steve Jones has to be punished along with the rest of them for what they did to me and for what they *will do* to others. But how and what can I do?

When I reached the end of the mall, I had somewhat of an idea.

In *Mein Kampf*, Hitler talked about the Jews as a sort of disease, a race rather than a religion. And although I know that this isn't true at all, I see his logic behind his explanation, the way he explains it so that others will swallow his propaganda the way they swallow a savory meal. The way Hitler views the Jews is the way I view The Clan. If he had known of and replaced the word "Jew" with "The Clan" then he would have hit the nail right on the head. In his reality, Hitler had to trump the Marxist and Jewish doctrines, and he had to do it with force. *"Terror is not broken by the mind, but by terror."* It makes sense—when have you ever heard of a situation when a robber was persuaded not to rob the very person they were robbing just because that person told them it wouldn't be worth it? That situation simply does not exist. A robber is only stopped by brute force, by fear. The police instill fear. Jail and trial is what the robber will face if caught—unpleasantries. An eye for an eye is the only way. This is what I realized as I was walking. The slow surge of thought finally sifted out the logic I must abide by. And it makes perfect sense. Why else would Steve Jones and Jordan Saunders be talking to John? Wasn't it John who stood up for himself by force? Wasn't it John who *pushed* (terror) the very person who *tripped* (terror) him? Even though that terror was not broken, the constrictions it held John by were. Now The Clan allowed John to talk to them and quite possibly even hang out with them—I have no idea if it's true but do I really think John was visiting his grandmother that late at night? I doubt it.

My movement against The Clan must be instilled with terror. How will I manage this? I haven't the slightest conception. I'm still lost. I'm going to close this entry now and finish *Mein Kampf*. Maybe when I do, I'll have a better understanding of what I must do.

~Peter

October 22, 20--

Sunday

I finished the book, and I'm astounded at the celerity at which I have read it. The bulk of it was a jumble of propaganda which I have basically outlined in my earlier entries, but weeded within was a bit of truth, or so as Hitler thought it. I'm still lost in regards to what I'm going to do and how I'm going to carry out *my* movement though.

Hitler's National Socialist Movement was carried out through long years of preparation and speeches in front of groups and groups of people. But not even that movement started off in a great hall flooded with people—it started out small. And so, even though I'm unsure of what I must do, I'm certain of this one fact: It must start out small as well. Rome wasn't built in a day, and if I've endured The Clan's bullying for this long, I think I can put up with it a little longer to get the ultimate revenge.

I can't let their stick sharpened at both ends scare me now.

Tomorrow is going to be the first day of the test. I'm going to wear my new attire and see how everybody treats me. I'd be dumbfounded if all it took for respect was a change in appearance. Somehow I don't think that it's going to be that easy.

~Peter

October 23, 20--
Monday

It didn't work and I caved.

I know how I told myself I'd hide my true feelings and not talk about school but having it bottled up inside was making me *physically* ill. I know I said that I've somehow transferred all the hurt into fury, but I think that I was just fooling myself. The hate was there, yes, but so was the condescending feeling I've grown to accept. I feel diminutive and don't think that anything I read or plan will ever get carried out.

Today, I told Dr. Murgelsy about her daughter. Her own daughter! I came right out and spilled my feelings for Katie. I cried in her mother's office, and her mother comforted me. (I didn't use Katie's real name. That much I kept to myself.) What I *did* elaborate upon was how a girl named "Kimberly" treated me, how at first she was nice and was partners with me until I found out she had a boyfriend (known as Larry to Dr. Murgelsy) that changed his girlfriend's attitude toward me, making her sneer and laugh every time I came to pass her in the hall and sit behind her.

It hurt me to bring these things up, but as soon as the words were out of my mouth I actually felt better. I was talking to Dr. Murgelsy about her own daughter without her knowing it, and she was agreeing that this girl sounded like a capricious and insensitive Plastic. She didn't come right out with those words, but hearing her agree with me made me feel fantastic.

I still didn't tell her about my situation in school and about The Clan and how I get beat up and picked on almost every day—I don't think I'm ready to tell her those things just yet, but maybe I don't need to establish a movement of my own after all, maybe all I really need is therapy. I'm already feeling slightly better about the whole Katie episode, and writing in my journal *does* help. But then again I don't know. There are still a lot of bad memories that are strapped around my heart, many open wounds that haven't healed yet, and if I don't act now will I ever? Probably not, and then The Clan will just continue their actions unto other innocent people, poisoning the minds of the humble girls they date—corrupting them. Corrupting all those around them who are stupid enough to listen.

Ugh, I'm trapped again.

Dr. Murgelsy questioned me about my change of wardrobe also, which brings me to what I started writing in the beginning of this entry: *It didn't work.*

I thought that everyone would notice the drastic change, but I was wrong—practically nobody realized it. And the ones that *did* realize it were the ones that I wish hadn't. You guessed it . . . The Clan. Before the bell rang, commencing Social Studies, Casey Vector came over, poked me in the side, and said, *"What's this, Jelly-rolls? Going Goth? Is your cream-filling black now?*" I spoke back and told him to "get bent." He recoiled and, after a moment's thought, twisted his mouth into a sneer. I saw John and the troubled look he had on his face; I think he knew as much as I knew what would later become of that. Speaking of John, I haven't really talked to him that much. I think my absence from hanging out with him over the past two weeks has taken its effect. I do see him in school and talk to him there a little, but it's not the same and we don't ever talk about or make fun of The Clan like we used to. I still talk to Tommy Boots as much as always and am delighted to say that he's the first of us to get a job—Carvel, couldn't you guess? It was him who first commented on my change of attire in Chem. I told him that I wanted to try something different and that I was sorry I didn't go out with him and John over the weekend. I think he understands. I see that look in his eye when John is around. He knows how I feel and what I think is happening.

But back to Dr. Murgelsy. She questioned me about the change also. I told her that it was my way of coping with the impending divorce. She nodded and said that it's understandable to go through a series of character changes when something as big as a divorce is dropped into your life. "Finding your inner self," she called it. She told me that she even went through this type of change and that it was perfectly natural and that I would "find myself" soon enough. Little does she know that the divorce has nothing to do with it.

Corolla and my parents asked about it as well. Corolla first, of course, and my parents almost at the end of dinner. I wasn't surprised that they didn't notice right away; they were too busy arguing with one another—something I've grown more accustomed to now. I told each of them at separate times (Corolla and my parents) that it was the new "style" in school and that I wanted to fit in with the crowd. They'd never know what the "in" thing was and wouldn't question it further. I thought Corolla, who has dressed me since before I could remember, might object, but she didn't. Neither did my mom; she only picked at her shepherd's pie and sneered at my dad who was asking me about my "new group of baseball friends."

I don't know why I just drew that, but it felt like the right thing to do. A picture is worth a thousand words. And in this case I guess it expresses the one thing that is still on my mind after this entry.

I only wish I was that thin.

~Peter

P.S. I intercepted a letter that was sent home today. It mentioned of the "slipping" of my grades. My parents will never receive it.

October 24, 20--
Tuesday

The Clan didn't waste any time.

I should have seen it coming.

I didn't.

It was after Mr. Clemmings's class that Steve Jones and Jordan Saunders dragged me out into the bathroom across the hall—that infamous bathroom which I've grown to hate. I twisted and writhed in their arms to escape but to no avail—they held me too tight.

John had left the classroom in sort of a hurry, which I found odd at the time, and when I was in the hall, I called out for his help. He was no more than ten feet away from me, walking in the opposite direction as if he didn't hear, but when I shouted his name he stopped for a moment and then continued on. My friendship with him is officially over now. At least I *tried* to help him when he endured the same type of abuse from The Clan. I even took a punch to the stomach for him and sat with him until he felt better, and all he could do in return was walk away from me? I *understand*: friendship. But for who?

In the bathroom, I was held up like John had been, except this time by Steve on my right and Jordan on my left.

In the middle, standing in front of me, was Casey Vector.

He stood stolidly and gazed at me with burning eyes. I saw a glint of a smile appear before I returned it with one of my own. I knew I had to face my fear, that terror was only broken by terror. That's when he punched me in the stomach. The air whooshed out of my lungs like a balloon with a hole in it—I think I even made a sound that resembled it—and I fell limp. Steve and Jordan continued to hold me. My dead weight in their arms must have been immense, but they somehow withstood it. Casey hit me three more times in the stomach and slapped me once in the face for good measure. I didn't feel it. My mind was elsewhere, envisioning what must be done. I was then kicked in the back and twice more in the stomach—those I felt. I fell to the tiled floor before their feet. Steve shifted over so that he was now in front of me, his eyes full of hate. Parting his lips, he instructed: *"Lick my shoes."*

I'd never give him the satisfaction. Instead, I spit on them. Probably the wrong thing to do if I wanted to avoid further injury, but the right thing to do if I wanted to start fighting back. I had to show them that I wasn't scared anymore (even though I was trembling). They noticed, and Steve spat right back at me and kicked me in the groin. I crawled over to the one of the urinals, the kind that descends all the way to the floor, and threw up. I think that's when one of them kicked me from behind, and my head smacked against the porcelain, knocking me unconscious for two periods.

I guess nobody came into the bathroom during that time,

or if they did, they didn't say anything, because nobody in The Clan got reprimanded for what they had done. I hadn't told on them and apparently nobody else had either. I'm probably going to wind up getting detention for "cutting" English now. I don't think Mrs. Foxwood would understand if I told her I had had "diarrhea" or some other stomach virus that confined me to the bathroom, forcing me to cut her class. Plus I don't think I'd want to risk everyone overhearing that excuse either. Just another thing to laugh at the fat and unloved Peter Rubin for—the loser who gets his education at Farmsville High School.

I bet Jordan and Casey were laughing it up in English when I didn't show. I know that one of them must have said something to Gary or Steve, because both of them were teasing me in Health, asking if I had a nice nap. I remember looking over to John that period.

John just looked away.

Before that, in French, Katie talked to me again. Though I kind of wish she hadn't. It wasn't like the first time and never would be. She swiveled around in her chair so that she faced me, and asked flat out: *"Why don't you just lick his shoes like he wants you to? He might stop beating you up."*

I felt like spitting on her like I had on Steve's shoes. It didn't take her any time at all to become corrupted. It's repugnant how she can be the seed of my psychologist, and be so easily manipulated to annex the very same persona that

Steve Jones has. Such a capricious Plastic.

Why don't I just lick his shoes? Why? *Why?* Because that would be giving in, handing him the knife to slit my throat with.

Throughout my whole life, I've been handing people the knife. Not anymore. I know what I must do now and it may seem very dark and very bestial but it's what has to be done.

I have to *kill* Steve Jones.

I have to kill him.

It's easier said than done, but if I don't do it, the situation I find myself in will only grow worse. I will continue to be treated with indignity. I will be spat on. I will be kicked.

Steve Jones has single-handedly ruined my life. He has taken my self-esteem, he has taken the moral excellence of Katie, and he has taken ONE HALF of my friends away from me, poisoning his mind and changing him within. John would never have allowed what happened to happen in the days before he began talking to Steve. And his great "plan" of getting The Clan to stop picking on me surely blew up in his face (if that was really his true plan at all). He's only a pawn in their chess game of life. He is en prise and will soon be taken. He no longer exists to me.

~Peter

October 25, 20--
Wednesday

He's dead.

I killed John.

Not in a somatic sense but in a world where only minds can exist. I ganked John's Toon in WOW. I'm not sure what drove me to do it—probably the fact that he turned his face away from me in Mr. Cane's class yesterday—but I did it just the same, and it felt *good!* No, it felt *great!* My Toon is OP, as I've already said, and since John's is only at level sixty-one, I slaughtered it. This all happened when I saw his Night Elf in the ganking area—Stranglethorn Vale—while I was farming honor points. And when I saw him, I knew exactly what I had to do.

I camped his body so that he couldn't rez (come back to life) but while I was doing that, a Dwarf, a Human, and two Gnomes appeared and attacked me. Somehow, I don't know how, I knew that these were John's new friends, maybe one of them was even Steve Jones himself—how I hoped it was. At first it looked as if I was winning, but then I realized that two of them were only feigning their deaths. Needless to say within five minutes, I decimated every one of them and then DC'ed (disconnected). Cyber-bullying? I think not. That's one medium where The Clan will never touch me.

Never.

If only I could have the powers my Toon possesses. It's not something that is possible but there is another way . . . make myself equal to or greater than the strength my adversary possesses. How? Additional artillery.

Since I'm not the athletic type, taking karate or some other form of martial arts is out of the question. And since I have no stamina anyway, I doubt that would have even worked. But there was a man by the name of Samuel Colt who invented something very equalizing.

It was the revolver.

I must buy a gun.

I'm not sure what led me to this decision—it might have been my Nerf gun sitting on my dresser—but now that I think of it, it is a *very* equalizing decision. Even the weakest fighter could win against the strongest as long as they possess a gun.

Thinking it over, I know I said yesterday that I have to kill Steve Jones, but when I flip back to that entry I see that I was just venting. I'm not sure I could actually bring myself to kill somebody. In the past, I had even thought it an immoral sin, but since I don't believe in god anymore, that argument can't hold water. I guess now I just wouldn't want to rob someone of their life, even if they are as deserving of it as Steve Jones is. If I did have a gun, though, The Clan would leave me alone. *"Terror is not broken by the mind, but by terror."*

After school, and keeping the thought in my mind, I

decided to ride my bike to Tower Records. There, I roved over the magazines that featured guns: *Gun Digest, Predator Xtreme, Guns & Ammo, Southern Sporting Journal.* Inside, I found a vast array of guns. There are shoulder guns and handguns, each with their own subcategories.

First, let me write what I learned about the shoulder guns. The term refers to rifles and shotguns that have five different methods of loading and unloading the bullets, or cartridges. These methods are called "actions," the first of which is called "bolt action." This works by a means of its own by inserting a cartridge into the firing chamber and removing the unfired cartridge after it's fired. All this is accomplished by a handle that sticks out to the side of the bolt, which the shooter must manipulate in a series of movements.

The next action is called "pump action." This method enters and ejects the cartridges into the firing chamber by way of a pump, which is located under the barrel of the gun. In order to eject the spent cartridge, the pump must be pulled backward toward the rear of the gun and then pushed forward toward the front. I pretty much knew about this action from watching old movies, especially *Terminator 2: Judgement Day,* where a biker cyborg pumps the shotgun with one hand—really hardcore.

Then there's "lever action," and from what I read is mostly used on rifles. This lever is exactly what its name suggests: a lever. It's located under and a bit behind the trigger and is used to eject a spent cartridge from the firing chamber by being pushed forward. When the lever is brought back into the firing position, it then loads a cartridge into the chamber—providing the "magazine," or bullet reservoir, isn't empty—and cocks the hammer so that the gun will be ready to fire again.

There are a lot of new terms that I'm still getting used to so bear with me. I actually had to write them on a separate piece of paper so that I wouldn't forget what they meant.

After lever action comes "semiautomatic," which I'm already familiar with because of my Nerf gun. The term refers to one cartridge being shot each time the trigger is pulled. The gun uses the energy from the firing of each cartridge to eject the empty case and insert the next cartridge into the gun's firing chamber. This is the main term I think of when I think of guns. This and automatic, which is the last action . . . I think.

"Automatic action" is designed the same as semiautomatic, save for one thing—the prefix. It is not semi; it's fully. As long as the trigger is held down, the gun shoots a cartridge—one after another, after another. How is this done? Search me, I'm still not sure yet, but with some more researching I'm sure I'll find out. There are probably a ton of forums online attributed to guns which I can look at.

Handguns pretty much follow these last two specific types of actions: semiautomatic and automatic. The latter of which is most seldom found. The only automatic handgun that I'm aware of is the machine handgun, or under its street name: *UZI*.

How do I get one of these, and which one will be right for me? I'm still not sure. Only time and more research will tell. But one thing is for certain: I will not stop until I know.

~Peter

October 26, 20--
Thursday

John gave me bad looks in Chem., and he completely ignored me in Social Studies and in Health. I have no doubt that it was in reference to me killing his Toon yesterday. I feel kind of bad when I think about it, but he brought it upon himself, didn't he? I'm having my doubts. Maybe he really *didn't* hear me calling his name in the hall. The fact that I saw him talking to Steve Jones that one time and hearing that story about him being over at his grandma's certainly could make me jump to conclusions. Maybe he was just too disquieted in Health to accept the fact that his new friends had beaten up his original best friend. I think I'm going to apologize to him tomorrow. Good friends are hard to come by and if I allow myself to distance him any further it will only increase his chances of being fully sucked in by The Clan. I talked to Tommy Boots about this in lunch and he agreed with me. That was five minutes before another juice carton sailed its way over and struck the wall, spraying us with apple juice. Tommy Boots went to the bathroom to wash it off, but I stayed put. I don't think I'll be using the school's bathrooms anymore this year.

In French, Katie flat out laughed at me when she saw that my pants still had some spray on them. She said, *"Aww, baby spill his juice?"*

I think Steve put her up to it because it looked as if she was struggling to get the words out. But she said it, and when she did, she laughed to herself. I bet it even felt good for her to make fun of someone. It's really a shame how my psychologist's daughter can be such an insensitive Plastic. No, pardon, *allow* herself to become one.

At home, over dinner, my parents fought again. I ate in silence and then quickly picked up my plate and left. When I was in the kitchen, I heard first a slap and then my dad shout at my mom for hitting him. My mom shouted back that she hadn't, that it was only him clapping his hands, knowing that I was in the next room, and that he was a "lying son of a bitch." It instantly brought back the memory of my mom coming into my room the night before I lost my journal and it made me want to tear my ears off. I can still hear them arguing now! This isn't something I want to be trapped in the middle of, but I fear it's not something that's up to me. The divorce is definitely going to happen soon enough—they're probably getting lawyers to draw up the papers even as I write this.

I think I'm going to go online and find a forum about handguns. I'm still set on the idea about getting one. I'm positive now that I don't want to kill Steve Jones, just scare him a bit. Scare him and his Clan into treating me with respect and watch them piss in their pants at the sight of a .45. I would gleefully trade both my Christmas and birthday presents for that one sight.

Two more months ’til Christmas. Maybe I’ll get my wish early.

~Peter

October 27, 20--
Friday

"FINAL SOLUTION."

It has to be done and now I'm sure of it: I have to KILL Steve Jones and the rest of The Clan. And while I'm at it, I'll kill everyone else their minds have poisoned as well. Which includes one by the name of Katie Murgelsy. Hitler talked about a "final solution," an extermination of the Jewish race. He got that part wrong, it wasn't the Jews at all but the pricks in the schools with the manipulating minds. Now I must implement my own final solution.

I guess you're wondering why my sudden change of mind since in yesterday's entry I wrote that I realized I was only blowing off anger. Let me tell you. *Oh, let me tell you!*

It started out in Social Studies; no, it started in Math. When I walked into the classroom I saw that someone—obviously Gary Reith—had written PETER RABBIT SUCKS COTTON TAIL! on the blackboard. By this point in my life it didn't faze me in the slightest, but what happened next did: Mr. Rugerdy walked in the room right behind me before I could erase it, and began laughing. I've never seen him laugh so hard, and it made my blood boil. I'm not positive if he knew right away whom it referred to, but the whole class did and when they saw Mr. Rugerdy laugh, it instantly split their sides. Giggling filled the room. Eruption upon eruption. The only person that was quiet was me—now making it pretty obvious to Mr. Rugerdy who the aspersion was intended for. And instead of saying something, he just erased it, laughing to himself, his eyes batting in my direction.

I think Mr. Rugerdy will be the first teacher to get a bullet if the staff tries to prevent me from doing what I have to do. And *certainly* Gary Reith will get his. I will definitely see to it that I send him to meet his dead father.

And that's not the worst of it by far; that's just me recounting and blowing off steam. Here's the rest:

Since I had it set in my head that I would apologize to John today, I tried to do just that. But he was late to Chem., and in Gym he was on Joe Kelly's team for volleyball and seemed to change rocket-fast before I could get to the locker room (another place I've grown to hate). By the time I finally caught up with him, it was in Mr. Clemmings's class, and Jordan Saunders wouldn't allow me to get a single word out. Every time I opened my mouth or tried to pass a note, he would throw something at me. I think that's when I first had the feeling that something bad was going to happen after class. But when class ended, and The Clan left, my fears were allayed.

I was just about to talk to John when Katie walked through the door. My first reaction was that she was coming to talk to Steve, but when I remembered that he had left and when she came up to me instead, it left me speechless. I was utterly shocked that she was talking to me. She said she had something to show me and that I needed to follow her to her locker. I should have been more vigilant but I guess she still has that effect on me. She said it had to do with her *boyfriend,* Steve, and myself and that it would be in my best interest to follow her before he saw that she was talking to me. I think I had taken one look back at John packing his backpack before I found myself walking out with Katie into the hall. In my mind then, I could have still talked to John in Health.

When Katie led me to a set of lockers across from the room, I knew something was suspicious. I had seen her at a locker in the adjacent hall once before, and it clicked that she was a decoy. No sooner than I realized it, Steve Jones popped out from behind two kids and dragged me into that god-forsaken bathroom again. Following him was Jordan Saunders, Casey Vector, Gary Reith, and *John Lombardi.* The last to come in was Katie. Casey and Jordan held me by the standard arm grip while I reeled and kicked my feet in an effort to escape. I didn't want to scream out; instead I wanted to tear each of their heads off, especially Katie's and John's. Neither of them deserves to live.

As I was doing this, I caught Steve out of my peripheral, leaning over toward John, whispering something in his ear. When he finished, he leaned over to Katie and kissed her on the cheek. She began to swoon but he steadied her and told her it would be okay. That's when I spit on her—it felt great to finally do it—and Steve rammed a fist into my stomach, causing me to choke and gasp for breath.

"Now you're going to get what you've got coming to ya!" Steve cackled with that twisted leer on his face. He motioned for John to move forward, and I saw that he reluctantly did so. A minute later he punched me in the eye.

It hurt, but not as much as my sorrow did. Here was one of my best friends, poisoned of mind, punching me in the eye. The very same friend—*fiend* I should now say—I was about to apologize to. How could I have been so blind?

After punching me, John began to swoon himself, but Steve and Gary clapped him on his shoulders, rewarding him with high-fives. He looked sick at what he had done, but I don't think he looked sorry.

Do I kill him, too?

Sadly this wasn't the end of my bathroom experience. Once John was out of the way, the rest of The Clan went to work on me. As I landed on the floor I coughed and spit out blood. It scared me horridly—I thought I was dying—before I realized the inside of my cheek was cut. Through gritted teeth I muttered, *"You'll be sorry!"* to Steve. In riposte he kicked me in the ribs and walked away.

Corolla immediately asked about my eye when I came home from school early. I told her that while I was playing baseball at lunch another "friend" called my name and I looked away from the ball. It hit me in the eye and I had to go to the nurse. Corolla didn't question the fact that the school "let me go home," she just assumed I'd never lie to her. I don't even think I could have stayed without the faculty questioning where my black eye came from anyway, and I certainly didn't want to stay to find out what The Clan would have to say. Them, or John. I hope that it drove a spike of remorse and regret into John's heart when he saw that I had cut because of what he had done to me.

Tommy Boots called me after school and asked why I wasn't in lunch. I told him that John would know and that I wouldn't be seeing either of them this weekend because of it. The weekend is going to pass fast but I hope it's enough time for my eye to heal. Already it's begun to blacken. If the blackness doesn't subside I know I'm never going to hear the end of it on Monday. But by Monday maybe I won't have to. Maybe by Monday I'll have something equalizing to instill the needed terror. No! To further terror unto death.

The kicker of the whole day was that my parents didn't even question my eye over dinner. I stayed with them for at total of five minutes before I couldn't stand their bickering and got up and left, locking myself in my room and writing this entry.

Dr. Murgelsy even asked me about my eye. My psychologist, whom I've known a little over a month, asks me about my eye while the two people I've lived with my whole life argued with one another while their injured son went unnoticed. Does that tell you something? It certainly tells me something.

When Dr. Murgelsy asked me about it I recounted the same lie I spun for Corolla. She swallowed it hook, line, and sinker and was happy that I was "making friends" through this trying time of my life, and said that I'd probably need friendship more than ever. In that sense, I guess I'm completely doomed since I don't have any now. Yeah I got Tommy Boots, but as long as he's with John or at Carvel (he works Friday nights and the weekends), he's as dead to me as John is.

Dead . . . Death . . . Death . . .

I honestly contemplated suicide tonight.

Prior to dinner I found myself in the bathroom, staring at my reflection in the mirror. Staring at the blackened eye that my ex-best-friend had caused. On the counter was my dad's razor and in the bathtub was a full basin of water. I'm not sure how long I stood there looking into my soul before I realized that I couldn't let The Clan get away with what they had done. If I killed myself it would only be one more of their victories in a long line to come.

Deciding my fate and that I would have to kill everyone in The Clan was the hardest decision I've ever had to make in my entire life.

Vincent Bivona

Thankfully I have renounced the belief of god and satan altogether. At least when I put a bullet in Steve Jones's head I will not be going to hell when I die.

~Peter

October 28, 20--
Saturday

I've decided to do it on Tuesday: Halloween.

I think it would be a perfect day for it. For one, the wearing of costumes in school would easily allow me to conceal a gun; for two, I could make an everlasting impression while I wear that Charles Manson mask to do it, which I might add, I picked up at the mall today. (For $39.95, I believe it was money well spent. An investment even.)

I spent the remainder of my day on the Internet searching information on where to get firearms, and while I was doing this, I found something called *The Anarchist Cookbook* by someone or something called The Jolly Roger. I downloaded it and found that it had an abundance of detailed information on the manufacturing of explosives and drugs. On one page I even found out how to make a pipe bomb!

Nothing at all is impossible, everything can be done if you only want it.

—Adolf Hitler.

The idea of settling the score with The Clan, and those that their minds have bastardized, may actually become a reality. My mind is set in stone, and with information like this

I *will* be able to achieve my goal.
    I want it. Nothing at all is impossible.

~Peter

October 29, 20--
Sunday

My mom noticed my eye at breakfast, and I told her that it happened yesterday while she was out—baseball with Tommy Boots and *John*. I think that lie will hold as long as she doesn't talk to Corolla, and I doubt that she'll talk to her about it anyway since they're rarely, if ever, under the roof at the same time.

My dad asked me—surprisingly since he hadn't since the summer—if I wanted to take a ride on the boat and maybe see if any Tuna were running. I told him that I would have liked to, but lied and said that I had a lot of schoolwork to catch up on. The reality being that I hadn't done a single shred of homework in the last month (I even ripped up the two notices the school sent home—I believe I mentioned one earlier in an entry). Instead, I delved deeper into my research on firearms and explosives.

I searched school shootings to try to get ideas, and I came up with a bunch of sights dedicated to the Santana High School shooting, the University of Texas massacre, the Bath School disaster, the Virginia Tech massacre, and the Columbine High School massacre. The latter, of which, I found the most information on.

It was a school-related shooting that was brought on by

two kids: Eric Harris and Dylan Klebold. In their rampage on their high school, they wounded twenty-three people and killed twelve. The Web site stated, in detail, how they carried out their plan of action, starting off by leaving an "I'm sorry video" for their parents, then strategically planting two twenty-pound propane bombs in duffel bags in their school's cafeteria. Their original plan was to wait in the parking lot for the bombs to detonate, and then shoot the students as they fled from the burning building. But one small problem occurred: the bombs didn't ignite. When this happened—or didn't for that matter—Eric Harris shouted, *"Go! Go!"* and he and Dylan pulled out their guns (Eric's gun of choice being a Carbine and Dylan's a Tec-9) and began shooting at the students outside as they made their way into the school. They killed few and injured more in this endeavor but mainly aroused suspicion of the "ruckus" they had just caused. From there, the two cleaved their way into the school's library where more shooting occurred. Here they asked everyone with a white hat to stand up, since wearing a white hat was the symbol of a jock—a.k.a. Steve Jones—and when none listened, they started shooting at random. Their undertaking ended when they finally decided to put a bullet in their own heads.

Throughout this whole episode, the two encountered two students whom they knew and let go free (Eric warning one: *"Brooks, I like you. Now, get out of here. Go home,"* and Dylan warning the other to leave the library after responding,

"Oh, just killing people" to the question of what he was doing). It made me think of Tommy Boots and *John.* I know I'd let Tommy Boots go free, but what about *John?* I can honestly say that I don't know. I really don't.

Let me state that even though martyrs like Eric Harris and Dylan Klebold had a solid idea, they still left too many variables open. For instance: Their plan was solely based on the detonation of the two propane bombs they set in the cafeteria, and when those didn't go off, they changed their plan and began shooting people at random.

I will do better.

First off, I won't be using a propane bomb for obvious reasons (no detonation times to misjudge). Instead, I will be using pure sodium from the Chem. lab. If I remember Mrs. Pastorelli's experiment, all I have to do is place it in water and *Voom!* instant destruction! (Thank you, Tommy Boots for the Chem. notes.) Second, I won't be doing this as my initial charge. If that were the case, then I would be alerting the whole school by setting off the fire alarms, which is pretty much what Eric and Dylan did when they stood outside shooting people at random. I will be doing it toward the end of my killing spree as a sort of a bonus to burn down the school so the atrocities of bullying will never happen again within those bricks.

Another point: I will not be shooting in wide-open spaces such as the cafeteria, the library, or outside. It leaves too much room for escape, and it will also alert those in the surrounding classrooms. And even though there is no way around alerting the other students, there *is* a way to secure the fact that I can kill as many of them as I can: I will go in succession from small classroom to small classroom, hovering just by the door and never fully entering; this way if they choose to run, I can level them with an automatic. I feel it'll be better this way if I stick to small confinements, plus the students will probably be cowering under their desks like in Columbine (since they already proved to be sloths in an evacuation during a rudimentary fire drill, just imagine them trying an exodus while their bodies are pumped full of fear; they'll be like deer, trapped in headlights, standing still until a bullet brings darkness), and all I'll have to do is prowl from classroom to classroom, chucking in pipe bombs to assure their bodily decimation and extinction of life.

The other thing that I realized was that for two people a kill count of twelve is atrocious. I'm saying this in the most respectful way I can, since I feel that Eric and Dylan probably endured the same abuse I have. But twelve? That's six students each! And not nearly enough! In one classroom, there sits twenty. I will learn from their mistakes and make sure that my shots count. I will not mistake injured students for dead. I will put a bullet in each of their heads even if they have been brought down by one to the heart. Reassurance is the key on that matter.

Also, I don't think I'm going to start off with a pipe bomb, which would be the most logical thing to do if I wanted to kill a lot of people, because if I did that then it might cause my main objective, the main purpose of my plan, to falter—to kill Steve Jones in the process. I do not want him escaping. And I certainly will not throw a pipe bomb in his room—I want to see him suffer, I want him to lick *my* shoes before he looks into my eyes, and I put a bullet between his.

To ensure his death, it would be prudent of me to start off the extermination in Mr. Clemmings's Social Studies class, since the majority of The Clan will be housed in there at that time. I'm well aware of the fact that it's possible that a few teachers, of whom I have no abhorrence towards, will be injured if they try to stop me in my *movement*. I cannot allow my mission to falter and for that I am sorry if I hurt them. The only reassurance I can grant myself is that I will not follow up with a subsequent shot to their heads. They will be the only ones I will leave for injured. Of all, Mr. Rugerdy will not be one of them.

As for making the bombs and buying the guns, I'm still behind on those matters. I better hurry since Halloween is in two days. I'm well aware that I'm going to have to find a proxy buyer that will allow me to purchase the guns through them, since I'm not of age and really don't have a clue where I can get them otherwise. But of course easier said than done. I've been searching blogs and forums on guns and might have found someone with the tag *ColtDancer666* who can help me.

We'll see if time is on my side.

~Peter

October 30, 20--
Monday

As is my luck, nothing goes the way I want it to.

I think I'm going to have to alter my original plan since *ColtDancer666* hasn't gotten back to me on the matter of the guns yet. Also, I think that when I do hear from him—*if* I hear from him and *if* he is the one to help me procure them—I'm going to change my order. I think it would be better to equip myself with small arms rather than the hi-point carbines and shotguns that Eric Harris and Dylan Klebold were known to carry in their arsenal. My thoughts on this matter came from doing research on Seung-Hui Cho, the shooter at Virginia Tech, who, as I will soon be, was a single gunman. He sported a Glock 19 and a Walther P22.

The smaller arms would allow me to be able to conceal and maneuver them easier. I'll have to be prudent in choosing which guns I'd want to straw purchase. I don't want to sport a .22 revolver like Charles Andrew Williams—another person I found a small blurb on—because of the small round capacity. I need them to be able to rip through person after person before I have to reload. Maybe I'll get a Smith and Wesson third generation .45 and a German Mauser M2. From what I've seen so far, I think they look pretty cool, and they're both semiautomatic. My allowance won't cover this, so I'll have to dip into my dad's stash. He keeps roughly twenty grand in the closet floor safe that I know the combination to. He only checks and deposits money in it on the twenty-eighth of every month, so on that note he won't figure out the "withdrawal" until after the deed is done.

I really feel that this is possible. At first, I was a little uneasy about it being a one- man operation, but if guys like Cho and Williams could go through with it—with Cho killing thirty-two people, more than twice that of Eric and Dylan combined—then so can I. *Nothing at all is impossible, everything can be done if you only want it.*

I want it! It will be possible!

On the note about the pipe bombs: I went to Home Depot today to buy the supplies. The clerks there were very helpful, and none of them were the wiser. I got the body for the pipe as well as the steel caps for the ends (course threaded as specified). Tomorrow I will get the filler that will be used for the explosive material and I will begin construction. As for fuses, I can simply rip the ones off the fireworks left over from the Fourth of July.

I also want to mention that, after Dr. Murgelsy's, I found two video games online to quell my anger of the school day and of not getting a response from *ColtDancer666*. The games are *Super Columbine Massacre RPG!* and *V-Tech Rampage* and are both based on the school shootings. I found *SCMRPG!* to be more fun than *V-Tech* because of all the integrated pictures and information on the massacre. The creator of the game really did his homework when programming it. There's even one part where Eric Harris meets Brooks in the parking lot and tells him that he likes him and that he should go home. It's crazy! And not that easy. I got caught sixteen times before I actually got past the setting of the bombs in the cafeteria, which, sadly, like in real life, didn't work out for them.

Since the game is an RPG, you don't really see too much bloodshed, but I still feel that I could relate to the characters and the shooters they portray. Maybe after I'm done with my movement, they'll make a game about me. I can only wonder.

I almost forgot to mention that there is a funny coincidence between the game and my life. In the game, Eric has a flashback of Dylan getting dry ice from his job at Carvel and making dry-ice bombs. When I saw this, I immediately thought of Tommy Boots and his new job. Maybe I could somehow manage to get dry ice from him to make a bomb. It'd sure be something cool to try, and I know *The Anarchist Cookbook* has a section in it about that. Or maybe I'm thinking too much. Sometimes less is more. I think the pipe bombs and the two handguns—if I can get them—will do. That and a hell of a lot of spare clips!

Dr. Murgelsy:

I think she had it set in her schedule today, or whatever she refers to, that she was going to talk to me about my parents and my ways of coping with their upcoming divorce. Despite the fact that I had already told her what I was doing to cope, she delved further, trying to unsheathe other ways. At first, I thought nothing of it but when she insisted, I immediately thought that maybe my parents had found my journal and had told her of my intentions. Her insisting transmuted into prying, and I was almost positive that she was trying to get me to confess my actions of coping, not only with my parents' divorce but with the tormenting I've undergone at school as well.

When she finally seemed propitiated from what I told her, my heart rate returned to its normal speed and I rationalized that if she really had known about my journal and my plans to eradicate the school—no, *exterminate* the school of its asinine population of tormenting cretins—then she would have done a lot more than just ask me rudimentary questions about my parents' divorce. It opened my eyes. When I'm finished with this entry, I'm going to hide my journal in a safer place other than that of *The Purloined Letter*. I think maybe I'll hide it inside my computer tower. Nobody will ever find it in there.

~Peter

October 31, 20--
Tuesday

Yeah, yeah, Happy Halloween.

:::Sarcasm:::

My plan would have been executed today if all had gone accordingly, but of course there have been setbacks.

Story of my life.

About those: The main one was *ColtDancer666*. I spoke with him again today, and he reassured me that he *can* help me with the transaction, but it has to be through this guy he knows instead of himself, and it will cost a little bit extra. I told him that price was of no issue, only time. He then mentioned that the earliest his friend could get the shotguns and rifles to me would be next Wednesday. I divulged that I was impatient and asked the time frame of acquiring small arms instead. I specifically mentioned the Mouser, the Smith and Wesson, and possibly an OTs-33 Pernach. It took him about an hour and a half to get back to me, but when he did, the delivery time was much better. He said that his friend could get the semiautomatics to him by this Thursday, but the automatic would have to wait until Monday; also I would have to meet him in a secure area for the transaction. Hearing this, I scratched the Pernach and said that the semiautomatics on Thursday would do just fine and suggested the grove of trees behind the Sun Valley Mall for our meeting. He agreed, and in two days, I will meet him there. That part at least I am ecstatic about.

The other concern on my mind is the pipe bombs, which of course can be accredited to none other than my own slothfulness in garnering the supplies and building them. I've decided that, since I'm now going to go through with my movement on Friday, I will have more time to build and test them—I guess the setbacks on the guns are a blessing in disguise; at least there's now a chance I can use the bombs. The only downfall to the short time frame will be that I'll have to build them simultaneously and hope that I get the construction right. I'll probably only have enough time to test their construction once and if they don't work then they're pretty much a bust.

I already started building them today and will continue after this entry. As I've mentioned yesterday, I already have the pipes and caps, and today I picked up the explosive material that will be used for the filler. It was easy to obtain since they're improvisions of gunpowder and were easily found in the chemical storage closet in Chem. class—hell, I killed two birds with one stone and grabbed the container of pure sodium while I was at it.

For the filler, I read that I can use either permanganate with sugar half-and-half or chlorate with sugar. I chose the chlorate since it has a higher explosive effect than the permanganate. I've adhered to the ratios precisely and mixed the parts. The compound is now sitting in the corner of my room, waiting to be housed within the steel tubing of the pipes. Once that's complete, all I have to do is thread the fuse through the tiny hole I drilled in the end cap, and *voilà!* Instant carnage! When that thing goes off, shrapnel will shatter the air and pierce walls, ceilings, and human flesh!

Revenge is at hand. I can almost taste it.

~Peter

November 1, 20--
Wednesday

Mrs. Pastorelli questioned our class today, stating that somebody in either our class, the one after, or during the five minutes between the period change had broken into the chemical storage cabinet and stolen both containers of sodium and chlorate. Since I waited until nobody was in the room to break it open, nobody could disclose any information. Tommy Boots had been absent yesterday—I'm not sure if I mentioned that or not—and *John* had left directly after the bell, probably to go brown-nose Steve Jones before Gym. Mrs. Pastorelli had gone out of the room to grab a cup of coffee as she always does between periods on "B" days, and the rest of the students had left as well. The crime was perfect, and nobody remembered that I was the last person out.

Despite the fact that she couldn't pin the wrap on anybody in our class, Mrs. Pastorelli said we were all suspects and that if she ever found out who did it then that person(s) will be subjected to legal action. Boo hoo hoo, little does she know that on Friday there will be plenty of legal action to go around.

On the note of the pipe bombs:

I finished building them last night and I tested one today, and it worked! It was a pretty nice-sized explosion from the sound of it—I certainly didn't pop my head up from the car door I was using as a shield to look. Revina's Clutch was a perfect place to test it and the scattered junk offered adequate protection from the shrapnel. Friday is going to be a field day!

Jordan Saunders poked me in the back again in English, and I couldn't help but smile. It's almost funny how he can't see the black shadow enshrouding him. When fourth period rolls around in two days he'll be well aware of it, and by that time it'll be far too late. It'll be too late for everyone.

I've taken a liking to *SCMRPG!,* and I've completed the library part and ended up in hell (suicide). I found more likenesses of the game to real life (Dylan Klebold to John Savage: *"Oh, just killing people."*), and I felt for Eric Harris when he had the flashback of Brenda Parker and his relationship with her. It reminded me of Katie Murgelsy, and it eased my pain to know that unlike Eric, I *will* get a chance to put a bullet in her head. Won't Dr. Murgelsy be surprised! I'm sorry to hurt her in the process since she has actually helped me ease a little of my pain through talking, but she even said it herself about her daughter—unknowingly of course—that Katie (Kimberly) sounded like a capricious and insensitive Plastic. Those were my words but she did imply them.

As far as the aftermath on Friday, I realize that I must succumb to suicide. I really hadn't thought about that part much—probably because I wasn't really sure if I would go through with it or not—but now I guess I should. It really is the best choice—NO MORE PAIN. The invitation sounds more than enticing; it sounds elegant. Plus, I wouldn't last in jail and that would be inevitable if I don't kill myself. Also, I couldn't see myself dealing with the moral and ethical judgment of what I will have done. It doesn't matter that god doesn't exist, I still, sadly, have a conscience, and being picked on, reading a book, playing video games, and planning my own movement will not diminish that fact. I simply will not be able to live with myself after what I will do in two days. And I *must* do this. Suicide is just something that has to be done as well.

They've left me no other option.

~Peter

November 2, 20--
Thursday

Tomorrow is the big day. Am I scared? A little. About dying? No, about failing.

What if Steve Jones is absent? It's one thought I hadn't considered until today. It would be deemed the ultimate FUBAR because I only have one chance at this, one shot to eradicate the world of mentally defective people like Steve Jones and receive my revenge for all that he has done to me. One shot. One chance. One ultimate gamble. And what is life but not a series of gambles? Are we not holding the dice every day, throwing them and wishing that snake eyes doesn't present itself like some inauspicious omen?

In a life where I have received the single malignant pips many of times, I feel that the odds are finally with me on my last roll. I can only hope that all will carry out as planned.

Over dinner, I saw my parents for what will be the last time. Halfway through the meal, I swallowed my suffering and told them that I loved them.

They didn't hear me over their arguing.

I left a message in my room for when they come home tomorrow and I don't. It confesses that I am sorry, not for what I will have done, but for having to leave them in such a gruesome way, and that none of it was because of them.

The impending divorce no doubt had an effect on my psyche, but nothing that can be compared to the years of abuse and torment that I have endured from people like Steve Jones and The Clan. I think Danny Ledonne, the creator of *SCMRPG!*, said it best: *"When you get pushed every day, and when you are ostracized not once, not twice, but years in and out, your perception of reality is distorted . . . These things really do warp your understanding and your perception of humanity in some almost irrevocable way."* I guess my reality has been distorted, but can you blame me? If the only thing you've come to learn is that when life gets you down, it spits on you further, countless times over and over again, then you start to develop a negative self-fulfilling prophecy of your subsistence that follows you throughout the rest of your existence. I've tried to stay positive—and if you've read this journal from entry one, you can see that I haven't always thought this way—but when your parents, whether it be intentional or not, a god that you once believed in, and life all spit on you, it leaves you no other choice. My pain has manifested into something that is too hard to live with; it gnaws at the very fabric of my will and emotion. Revenge and death are the only ways out. Suicide is just one thing more that I must endure but will be well worth it to put The Clan and all who follow them to death.

On that note I will gladly write that I met with *ColtDancer666* in the grove of trees today at the Sun Valley

Mall. He delivered the Mouser and the Smith and Wesson, and we gladly made our exchange—money for the means of impending death. The guns are heavier than I expected but not a burden to bear. I feel a sense of alchemic vigor surge through my veins when I wield them. I feel in power! With that I will leave you with one last story I wrote, dedicated especially for what will unfold tomorrow:

THE DAY OF DAYS

BY PETER RUBIN

Peter Rubin stalked from classroom to classroom with his Smith and Wesson .45 drawn, looking for Steve Jones. There was a hollow-tipped bullet with his name on it, and Peter felt his livelihood was to deliver it unto him.

The .45 felt heavy. The backpack concealing the pipe bombs, heavier still. With a dexterous agility that can only be attributed to playing countless hours of video games, Peter swapped the .45 for a pipe bomb. In his right hand he now held a lighter. The fuse stood in fey, eagerly awaiting its sole purpose of existence. Peter struck the lighter, the flame danced and soon kissed the fuse. A silent scream escaped as it dwindled down in stature and the pipe found itself sailing through the air into an open classroom. When it struck the ground it announced itself as a dud—too little filler and not a long enough fuse.

Peter frowned.

It didn't worry him much. The classroom in which the failed attempt at a bomb rested was not the main objective: the one two doors down was. Grimacing at the thought of Steve Jones sitting at his desk, alive, Peter walked on, drawing both the .45 and the Mouser again.

::Knock, knock, knock::

The sound was heard over the screams, which now pierced the air. Behind him, the students in the classroom had figured out the barbarous pipe's failed intentions and were beginning to flee into the hall. Peter paid little attention to them, instead focused only on Mr. Clemmings and his class. Mr. Clemmings, the teacher who had always left the room at the most inopportune moments. After today, he would never leave again.

"Knock, knock, knock," Peter shouted, wielding the Mouser in his right hand and firing a bullet into the ceiling tiles. A fluorescent light exploded and shattered through its casing onto the floor. Peter smiled—the sound of destruction delighted him.

"Steve Jones!" he boisterously called out. "Stand up!"

His command reminded him of Eric Harris's, where the gunman instructed everyone in a white baseball hat to stand up, and that made him smile further. He leered with deranged glee and cackled loudly.

"Steve Jones, stand up!" he repeated.

Finally, after much hesitation, Steve Jones did *stand. Peter then replaced the .45 and lit a second pipe bomb and flung it out into the hall full of screaming students. It exploded seconds after it left his hand and transformed itself into searing shrapnel that lodged itself into the soft tissue of fleeing bodies. Lacerations were made, eyes were pierced, and oozed white liquid, and heads were cleaved open, spilling brain, blood, and cerebral fluid onto the tiled floor. Peter didn't notice any of this; his gaze was too steadily focused on the visage of Steve Jones. The leader of The Clan sensed his impending death and a section of denim at the fork of his pants darkened. If this had been a normal school day, Peter would have been ecstatic to see his worst nightmare soil himself. Today, it didn't matter. Today, it eased him not.*

He closed the gap between himself and Steve Jones and fired bullets into the bodies and heads of the cowering classmates he once shared the school with. Each of them fell to the ground in a loud THUNK! *and stained the floor a dark-red, almost black, their blood pooling together to form one big macroscopic puddle of death. They all had laughed at him at one point in their insignificant lives, and they all deserved to die. Steve Jones, however, would get it special. He was their ringleader.*

"What . . . what are you going to do to me?" he asked, begging for his life.

Peter Rubin just looked at him, unblinking. "Lick my shoes," he said after much thought.

"Wha—what?"

"Lick my goddamn *shoes!" Peter demanded.*

Steve dropped to both knees and did so.

A diminutive feeling of satisfaction rippled across the emotional coat Peter wore, but from the years of abuse, kicks, rips, and tatters he had endured from The Clan, the feeling washed over him unfulfilled. Something much darker and much more serious would have to be done to appease his urges.

Firing the Mouser twice more—one striking Mr. Clemmings in the left eye, decimating it into oblivion, and another casting the cloven head of Sally Rutchfield onto the floor—and listening to the blowback of the hammer, he surmised an idea.

"Stand up!" Peter shouted his commands with stern authority. The hurt of old wounds was resurfacing and he had to placate his anger before something like grief overcame him.

Steve Jones stood up.

With one swift kick, Peter's shoe found a home between Steve Jones's darkened pants, sprawling him out on the floor, making him grab at his crotch. Peter then extracted the pair of handcuffs he brought and secured Steve to Mr. Clemmings's desk while he himself exited the classroom, firing off round after round into students' heads and casting pipe bombs into the surrounding classrooms. After twenty minutes and a full out slaughter had been beheld in his eyes, he returned to Steve Jones.

"Now to die like the dog you are! Kneel!"

Steve Jones did as he was bade, and, as Peter looked into his crying eyes—his own set ablaze—he ascertained that the boy on his knees before him was morally sorry for what he had done. Nevertheless, he was a day late and a dollar short. Peter lifted both the Mouser and the Smith and Wesson .45 and shattered both of Steve's knees at the same moment. The jock reeled to the floor, screaming, before Peter placed two more bullets in his feet. Blood began to torrent onto the floor, joining his fellow classmates' in that all-too-familiar hodgepodge of liquid death. The bully's screams pierced Peter's ears but they were music, a harmony of blissfully sweet retribution. Steve Jones writhed in pain for a full five minutes before the very person he tormented year in and year out finally decided to end the bully's life with a point blank shot to the head. Peter executed this by picking the wriggling worm up by his hair and pressing the muzzle of the .45 into his cheekbone. The crack of the pistol was loud and the back of the worm's head exploded in a cloud of grey and sanguine mist.

Peter Rubin's revenge was complete.

He then cast the .45 away, knowing no other solution to escape the grief that would befall upon him, and stuck the Mouser in his mouth. He wouldn't die by the same gun that killed Steve Jones; he'd never afford the dead cretin that much pleasure. As he tasted the hot steel and tongued the bore of the barrel, a single-worded-thought flashed across his mind before he squeezed the trigger and all went blank:

Vengeance.

It really is a shame; I could have been a writer. I could have been a lot of things, but I was led to believe otherwise. I have to do what I'm about to do. There is no other option.

The only thing I regret is that I have not done this sooner.

Steve Jones's world will soon be replaced by neither blackness nor whiteness—but by nihility.

Goodbye.

~Peter Wade Rubin

November 2, 20--
Entry 2

You've got to be kidding me!

After writing what I was hoping to be my concluding entry, I decided to play WOW one last time and bumped into Tommy Boots's Toon. I whispered to him to get in Vent, and when he did I bade him not to go to school tomorrow. I hadn't made up my mind if I was going to tell him or not, but when I got the opportunity to talk to him, I decided I would ask him to stay home. He asked me why, and I told him I couldn't tell. He seemed reluctant not to ask again, but said he would do as I asked, as long as he could get in touch with *John.* My face twisted into something of enmity when I heard the mention of that betrayer's name, but I didn't reject Tommy Boots's plea. If Eric Harris could reconcile a friendship with Brooks Brown so that Dylan Klebold would not be torn between them, then I can do the same to save Tommy Boots's life. He has always been there for me, and I wouldn't want him to suffer through any of this more than he has to. Maybe after my death, he'll think of me and all the abuse we both endured from The Clan and be happy to realize that I finally got the ultimate revenge. Maybe not. That doesn't matter, and I wish not to think of that anymore for it may flag my intentions. What I will say is this: I'm furious at the fact that *John* didn't pick up either his cell or house phone when Tommy Boots called him. Whether he is out with The Clan or out with his parents on a school night, I care not—I only care about my revenge. Which I will now have to postpone yet again. Another snake-eyes for the time being!

I instructed Tommy Boots NOT to mention any of our conversation to *John* until Sunday, since D-day has now moved to Monday. By doing that at least I will be certain that he can't go back and tell Steve Jones not to come in. Now my doubts are growing on that matter and I'm becoming more and more impatient. Maybe I should have left Tommy Boots in the blind, maybe that would have been better.

I don't know anymore. Everything is falling apart at the very end.

~Peter

November 3, 20--
Friday

I didn't go through with it since I'm obviously still writing. And Steve Jones *was* in school today, so it's a real pity I didn't. The only thing I can do is hope that Monday will play out the same. Last night I thought long and hard about cutting school today and finally decided that if I did then it would raise further suspicion in Tommy Boots's mind and that would not be good. I need him to stay calm and uncertain. If he really wants *John* safe then he'll tell him on Sunday night like I asked. But if he has even the slightest of guesses of what I'm planning to do he'll blow my cover to save my life—that I am sure of. It's just his caring nature.

I don't want to talk about school since I feel it's better to remember everyone as they are. And I don't want to talk bout Dr. Murgelsy since I'm going to kill her daughter, but I feel that I have to because of what we talked about.

I was sitting in the familiar leather armchair as I always did when she asked me, *"Peter, are you happy?"* Looking at it now it was probably just an inquisitive question, but at the time I thought more of it, a lot more. It seemed that she saw into the depths of my soul, as if my skin had turned transparent and she could see the morbid thoughts and feelings that I now possess and cannot rid myself of. Struggling to lie to her, I found that I couldn't, and before I knew it I was saying the words: *"No, I'm not."* I immediately bit my tongue and held back a shriek of pain. My eyes watered from it but she thankfully mistook it for crying and gave me a tissue. The next forty minutes of our time was dedicated to delving into why I was unhappy. This, thankfully, I found that, in a sense, I *could* lie about. I managed to hide my feelings on being picked on my whole life and about my movement, but spilled my guts on the matter of my parents and how I don't think they recognized me anymore, how they're possessed more in their arguing than in rekindling what may be their last chance at saving their marriage.

I didn't expect it but Dr. Murgelsy made me feel slightly better on that matter as she had before when I was truthful with her. Looking back, I'm just glad that our time together expired before I could disclose any more information, because if we had just one more hour I believe I would have exposed *everything*.

Today was too close. My firm hold on my emotions is slipping.

———

~Peter

November 4, 20--
Saturday

Once again: a blessing in disguise.

I'm glad now that Tommy Boots couldn't get in touch with *John* because this afternoon I decided to go out to Revina's Clutch again and test fire both the Smith and Wesson and the Mouser. To my surprise, the recoil on them was more than I expected, and they ripped free from my loose grip. If that had happened at school then I might have had to kiss everything goodbye. Anybody with enough intrepidity could have picked them up and ended my movement in one swift movement of their own.

After retrieving them and squeezing off a few rounds on each, I grew accustomed to their recoil, and I can now say with confidence that that will not happen on Monday. I left Revina's Clutch shortly after, not wanting to overstay my welcome. It's in a pretty remote area—which will silence the gunshots—but kids still go there to ride their bikes and I didn't want to risk being seen. When I returned home, I placed the guns with their reloaded magazines and extra clips in my computer tower where they will sit until Monday morning.

I thought about spending some time with Corolla, kind of like saying my last goodbyes, then thought better of it. The less I see of anyone now the better. I will stay in seclusion until I am reborn like the great phoenix from the ashes of the flame.

I am now patient. I am certain. I have a firm grip on my reality.

~Peter

November 5, 20--
Sunday

This is my second time writing it but: *Tomorrow is the big day!*

Everything is ready.

I've packed my backpack with the twelve remaining pipe bombs and two lighters. I've reloaded and double-checked the magazines of the semiautomatics that I will tuck into my belt. And I've loaded their extra clips to full capacity—twenty in all. I want to waste nothing that I have purchased; I plan to rip through every last cartridge before I put that final bullet in my head, ending my pain, torture, and suffering.

This has been long overdue.

Every time I close my eyes, my mind is bombarded by a collage of pictures consisting of Eric Harris, Dylan Klebold, Seung-Hui Cho, Kip Kinkel, Charles Whitman, and the blurred, screaming faces of all of whom I will kill.

All these years of torment finally taking their toll on my soul.

I want to see everyone cower before the one person they never expected to retaliate. Furthermore, I want to see The Clan themselves trembling at my feet as they beg for their lives. I want to see the pupils of Steve Jones prior to making him lick my shoes and prior to putting a bullet in his brain, fracturing his skull and scattering his blood about the floor. I want to see the look on Katie Murgelsy's face as I do this to her boyfriend—before I do it to her.

I want to be *that* guy. I want to succeed. I want my revenge.

I need only one good roll of the dice.

My time is now.

I am ready.

I have transferred my pain and my fury onto the page and all that remains is my resolve.

~Peter Wade Rubin

Peter Rubin's Journal
End's Here

AFTERWORD

Even though the names and places in this novel are a work of fiction, the ideas, the hazing, and the thoughts and feelings instilled are not. I want to make it clear that at least one student in every school is keeping a journal like the one you have just read. That person may never escalate to the degree of retaliation that Peter Rubin has, but then again they may. I wish to make it evident that it is bullying in the schools, as well as the surrounding elements in our students' lives, that contribute to depression and feelings of worthlessness. This can, and often does, lead to suicide, but in some circumstances a mass murder precedes it.

Bullying is one prevalent factor that has been overlooked and underestimated. It is stated in Bullying Behaviors Among US Youth: Prevalence and Association With Psychosocial Adjustment by T.R. Nansel, M. Overpeck, R.S. Pilla, W.J. Ruan, B. Simons-Morton, and P. Scheldt, that almost 30 percent of youths in the United States (over 5.7 million) are estimated to be involved in bullying as either a bully, a target of bullying, or both. In a recent national survey of students in grades six to ten, 13 percent reported bullying others, 11 percent reported being the target of bullies, and another 6 percent said they bullied others and were bullied themselves.

These youths being bullied have succumbed to many of the atrocities that Peter Rubin has faced. We as a society must become aware of the potency in the "disses" that we administer throughout the school day and in our lives. Not everybody is apt to take it as something to evoke laughter upon themselves; conversely, many take these disses as damaging aspersions, which, I would like to add, are usually their intentions.

I have written this, as well as the work of literature that precedes this, to request that you, and all who you know, please think before you decide to call someone a name, throw a paper airplane, or draw a picture on a blackboard because you never know how it will affect the person whom it is directed toward. Not everyone is built of a solid foundation, and not everyone is free from the heckling clutches of bullies and their crude tormenting the rest of the year. These students may, and may have already, endured suffering and anguish throughout their whole existence. Not everyone is the same, but everyone deserves the chance to be treated the same.

The word is EQUALITY, and we should embrace it rather than shun it.

Arm yourselves with knowledge: The old aphorism "Sticks and stones will break my bones, but words will never hurt me," does not hold water; words do hurt; words can kill.

AUTHOR'S NOTE

While writing *The Journal of Peter Rubin,* I actually began slipping into a period of depression. I endured a multitude of unceasing migraines of which I have never encountered before. While focusing on these occurrences, and feeling them for what they actually were instead of suppressing them with an aspirin tablet, I grew a small understanding of constant physical and mental anguish. I can only imagine what Peter Rubin, and one in his position, would have felt before succumbing to a mass murder and suicide; his suffering would have been incessant throughout his whole life rather than a short epoch, and it would have been pure torture.

The following pages of this book were meant to contain a prayer and a poem for each school-related shooting. However, there are too many separate instances to list so I feel that I will instead leave you with one poem dedicated to everyone as a whole who have lost their lives (and for everyone that will, sadly, lose their lives to ones in the future if an end is not put to this way of coping).

It is up to us, not to arm ourselves with semiautomatic weapons, but to arm ourselves with the power of mind to stop bullying our fellow classmates and people we walk the earth with, to feel for them and realize that everyone is born into the world the same: naked and with a clean slate.

We are all equal, and we should be treated and treat others as we wish to be treated ourselves.

~Vincent Bivona

Please do not believe that the past has left me:
Simply because it is not my friend;
Please do not believe that I am whole:
Because I never shall be again.

My memories haunt me in my sleep,
They haunt me when I am awake;
Some say be thankful for what is left,
But my memories are something I can no longer take.

I am now a broken vessel,
One that can no longer float;
This coat of emotion I wear is torn;
And I shall never again gloat.

I look to the sky for solace,
And I see the faces of my loved ones gone;
I try to find the jubilance I once felt,
And once again those emotions abscond.

I seek the Lord for consolation,
High above the firmament;
But despite His assuring words,
I shall forever . . . lament.

—Diane Daniels

THE JOURNAL OF PETER RUBIN . . .

For more information regarding Vincent Bivona
and his work, visit his Website:
www.VincentBivona.com.

Further copies of this book may be
purchased online via LegworkTeam.com;
Amazon.com; BarnesandNoble.com;
or Borders.com.

You can also obtain a copy by ordering it from
your favorite bookstore.

Vincent Bivona encourages his readers to view his
website and invite him, via e-mail, to book club events.
He is very passionate about his work and would
love to meet and discuss the central elements
contained within the story's plot.

Printed in the United States
125745LV00001B/70-72/P